The Home Owner's Journal:

What I Did and When I Did It

By Colleen Jenkins

Fourth Edition

CONFLUENCE PUBLISHERS, INC.
2232 N. 7th Street, Suite 15
Grand Junction, CO 81501
www.homeownersjournal.com

The Home Owner's Journal:
What I Did and When I Did It

By Colleen Jenkins

Fourth Edition

Cover Design and Illustrations by Julia Schreifels

Printed in the United States of America

Published by:

CONFLUENCE PUBLISHERS, INC.
2232 N. 7th Street, Suite 15
Grand Junction, CO 81501
(970) 257-0606
(800) 444-5450
www.homeownersjournal.com

ISBN 0-9725591-0-8

57   56   55   54   53   52   51   50   49   48   47   46   45

TABLE OF CONTENTS

THANK YOU ! ! !

At the request of the publisher, I kept a running list of every person who contributed to this book. When the book was finally ready for press and we looked over the list, I was amazed that more than ninety people contributed! A big THANK YOU to all of you!

IMPORTANT PERSONAL PAPERS

List your important personal papers and where they are kept. Examples are your will, life insurance policies, fire insurance policies, stocks and bonds. Also list the location of your safe deposit box and all bank accounts. Include policy limits and the name of your attorney, agents, and brokers, etc. Tell your emergency contact person(s) about this book and where it can be found.

Item	Details

HOW TO USE YOUR JOURNAL

This is the book I wish I had when we first bought our home forty years ago. I don't know how I managed without it. The fact is, I did not manage well at all. In all those years, I finally made the same mistake one too many times and decided to find a solution. I don't recall the precise instant, but it was either when I recently wallpapered the bathroom or when I painted the outside of the house.

The consequence of my failure to write down how much paint I used the last time was two gallons of custom mixed, non-returnable, paint (which is now considered hazardous waste) left over after I finished painting the house. Had I written down the amount I used the previous time, I would have saved myself time and money! When I estimated how often things like that probably happened in the more than forty years I have lived in my home, the need for this book became painfully clear. Believe me, I do NOT have money or time to waste.

I thought this book would be simple to do, but I actually wrote many drafts before arriving at what I think is a very practical, easy-to-use, and flexible journal. Since no two homes are alike, complete only the sections that are applicable to your home. I suggest making all entries in pencil. This will allow you to easily make corrections and updates.

This book has 11 main chapters. The sections within each chapter are organized in alphabetical order, except where items have special relationships to each other.

Most main sections end with lined space for extra notes. These note segments can also be used as graph paper for drawings, etc. You may want to sketch the walls and show window and door measurements, wiring projects, or make notes about what to consider next time. Some sections are comprised of only a heading and lined paper for writing or drawing. This maximizes flexibility and enables you to tailor the section to fit your particular needs.

Good luck! Let me know what you think of the book and how we can improve it. As always, suggestions from readers were incorporated into this edition. Maybe your suggestions will be in the next!

Colleen Jenkins, Author

PURCHASE, FINANCE, & INSURANCE

PURCHASE INFORMATION

Date We Moved In *June 25, 2003* _____ Square Ft. of Home _____

Property Legal Description (block, lot no., etc.) _____

Lot Marker Locations _____

_____

_____

_____

Builder/Contractor's Company _____

    Contact Person _____ Phone _____

    Date Home Built (completed) _____

    Warranty on Construction _____

Land Development Company _____

    Contact Person _____ Phone _____

Real Estate Company _____

    Agent _____

      Office Phone _____ Cell Phone _____

Notes: _____

_____

FINANCE INFORMATION

Mortgage Company _____ Loan Officer _____

    Office Phone _____ Cell Phone _____

    Loan No. _____

    Loan Servicing Dept. Phone _____

New Mortgage Company (if your mortgage is sold) _____

    Loan No. _____

    Phone _____ Date Sold _____

    Mortgage Balance at Time of Sale _____

Notes: _____

_____

_____

9

Second Mortgage Company _____

    Phone _____

    Loan No. _____

    Date _____

    Balance of Principal on Original _____

Mortgage Information

    Purchase Price _____ Price Asked _____

    Downpayment _____ Appraised Value _____

    Mortgage Amount _____ Location of Abstract _____

    Mortgage Type (FHA, VA, Conventional, etc.) _____

    Interest Rate (beginning, if adjustable*) _____

    Terms (30 yr. fixed, adjustable*, etc.) _____

    Points (no. & $ amount) _____

    Realtor's Commission (% & $) _____

    Other Closing Costs _____

    Closing Date _____

*Adjustable Rate Mortgage (ARM) Information

Rate	Date of Change	Principal Remaining	Monthly P & I

PURCHASE, FINANCE, & INSURANCE (continued)

Adjustment Interval _____

Index _____

Margin _____

Interest Rate Caps (yearly, lifetime, etc.) _____

_____

Monthly Payment Cap _____

Graduated Payments _____

Negative Amortization (y/n & limit) _____

"Introductory" Rate _____

Assumability _____

Convertibility _____

Prepayment Privilege _____

Points (including origination fee) _____

Other _____

INSURANCE INFORMATION

Title Insurance Company _____

   Title Binder No. _____

Homeowner's Insurance Company _____

   Agent's Name _____

   Office Phone _____ Cell Phone _____

   Policy No. _____

   Expiration Date (Month & Day) _____

Notes: _____

_____

_____

_____

_____

_____

_____

_____

_____

11

ATTIC

(Use tick marks at top & bottom to make graph paper)

BASEMENT

(Use tick marks at top & bottom to make graph paper)

BATHROOM NUMBER I

FLOOR COVERING

Floor Measurements

Widest part of room from middle of doorway _____

Longest part of room from middle of doorway _____

Notes: _____

_____

Type & Material (nylon carpet, ceramic tile, etc.) _____

Purchased From _____ Date _____

    Brand & Pattern _____

    Color & No. _____ Warranty Period _____

    Type of Backing _____ Pad Type _____

    Cost/Unit $_____ No. of Units _____ Total $_____

Installed By _____ Attached With _____

    Date _____ Cost $_____

Cleaned/Refinished By _____

    Date 1 _____ Cost $_____

    Date 2 _____ Cost $_____

    Date 3 _____ Cost $_____

Notes: _____

_____

CEILING COVERING

Type of Covering (paint, spray texture, etc.) _____

Purchased From _____ Date _____

    Brand & Pattern _____

    Color & No. _____ Warranty Period _____

    Applied with (texture roller, sprayer, etc.) _____

    Cost/Unit $_____ No. of Units _____ Total $_____

Installed By _____

    Date _____ Cost $_____

Notes: _____

_____

14

WINDOW COVERING

Window 1 Measurements

Height _____ Width _____ Top of Window to Floor _____ Trim Width _____

Type of Covering (draperies, blinds, etc.) _____

Purchased From _____ Cost $_____ Date _____

    Measurements of Window Covering _____

    Material & Cleaning Instructions _____

Cleaned By _____ Cost $_____ Date _____

Cleaned By _____ Cost $_____ Date _____

Notes: _____

_____

Window 2 Measurements

Height _____ Width _____ Top of Window to Floor _____ Trim Width _____

Type of Covering (draperies, blinds, etc.) _____

Purchased From _____ Cost $_____ Date _____

    Measurements of Window Covering _____

    Material & Cleaning Instructions _____

Cleaned By _____ Cost $_____ Date _____

Notes: _____

WALL COVERING

Wall Measurements

    North _____ South _____ East _____ West _____

Use "2nd Type of Covering" for woodwork or paneling. It has a "Refinished By" section.

1st Type of Covering (paint, paper, etc.) _____

Purchased From _____ Date _____

    Brand & Pattern _____

    Color & No. _____ Warranty Period _____

    Cost/Unit $_____ No. of Units _____ Total $_____

Installed By _____

    Date _____ Cost $_____

Notes: _____

_____

WALL COVERING (continued)

2nd **Type of Covering** (woodwork, paneling, etc.) _____

Purchased From _____ Date _____

   Brand & Pattern _____

   Color & No. _____ Warranty Period _____

   Cost/Unit $_____ No. of Units _____ Total $_____

Installed By _____

   Date _____ Cost $_____

Refinished By _____

   Date _____ Cost $_____

Notes: _____

_____

SAMPLES: PAINT, WALLPAPER, ETC.

attach swatch or paint daub here

FURNITURE/FIXTURES

Item	Purchased From	Date	Cost	Warranty

DOORS/TRIM

Purchased From _____ Date _____

    Brand & Style _____ Material (oak, steel, etc.)_____

    Stain/Paint Color & No. _____

      Finished With (polyurethane over stain, etc.) _____

Installed By _____ Total Cost $_____

Refinished By _____

    Refinished With _____

    Date _____ Cost $_____

Hardware Description _____

_____

    Purchased From _____ Date _____

    Cost/Unit $_____ No. of Units _____ Total $_____

Notes: _____

_____

EXTRA NOTES

(Use tick marks at top & bottom to make graph paper)

BATHROOM NUMBER 2

FLOOR COVERING

<u>Floor Measurements</u>

Widest part of room from middle of doorway _____

Longest part of room from middle of doorway _____

Notes: _____

_____

<u>Type & Material</u> (nylon carpet, ceramic tile, etc.) _____

Purchased From _____ Date _____

Brand & Pattern _____

Color & No. _____ Warranty Period _____

Type of Backing _____ Pad Type _____

Cost/Unit $_____ No. of Units _____ Total $_____

Installed By _____ Attached With _____

Date _____ Cost $_____

Cleaned/Refinished By _____

Date 1 _____ Cost $_____

Date 2 _____ Cost $_____

Date 3 _____ Cost $_____

Notes: _____

CEILING COVERING

<u>Type of Covering</u> (paint, spray texture, etc.) _____

Purchased From _____ Date _____

Brand & Pattern _____

Color & No. _____ Warranty Period _____

Applied with (texture roller, sprayer, etc.) _____

Cost/Unit $_____ No. of Units _____ Total $_____

Installed By _____

Date _____ Cost $_____

Notes: _____

WINDOW COVERING

Window 1 Measurements

Height _____ Width _____ Top of Window to Floor _____ Trim Width _____

Type of Covering (draperies, blinds, etc.) _____

Purchased From _____ Cost $_____ Date _____

   Measurements of Window Covering _____

   Material & Cleaning Instructions _____

Cleaned By _____ Cost $_____ Date _____

Cleaned By _____ Cost $_____ Date _____

Notes: _____

_____

Window 2 Measurements

Height _____ Width _____ Top of Window to Floor _____ Trim Width _____

Type of Covering (draperies, blinds, etc.) _____

Purchased From _____ Cost $_____ Date _____

   Measurements of Window Covering _____

   Material & Cleaning Instructions _____

Cleaned By _____ Cost $_____ Date _____

Notes: _____

WALL COVERING

Wall Measurements

   North _____ South _____ East _____ West _____

Use "2nd Type of Covering" for woodwork or paneling. It has a "Refinished By" section.

1st Type of Covering (paint, paper, etc.) _____

Purchased From _____ Date _____

   Brand & Pattern _____

   Color & No. _____ Warranty Period _____

   Cost/Unit $_____ No. of Units _____ Total $_____

Installed By _____

   Date _____ Cost $_____

Notes: _____

_____

WALL COVERING (continued)

2<u>**nd**</u> **Type of Covering** (woodwork, paneling, etc.) _____

Purchased From _____ Date _____

   Brand & Pattern _____

   Color & No. _____ Warranty Period _____

   Cost/Unit $_____ No. of Units _____ Total $_____

Installed By _____

   Date _____ Cost $_____

Refinished By _____

   Date _____ Cost $_____

Notes: _____

_____

SAMPLES: PAINT, WALLPAPER, ETC.

attach swatch or paint daub here

FURNITURE/FIXTURES

Item	Purchased From	Date	Cost	Warranty

DOORS/TRIM

Purchased From _____ Date _____

   Brand & Style _____ Material (oak, steel, etc.)_____

   Stain/Paint Color & No. _____

     Finished With (polyurethane over stain, etc.) _____

Installed By _____ Total Cost $_____

Refinished By _____

   Refinished With _____

   Date _____ Cost $_____

Hardware Description _____

_____

   Purchased From _____ Date _____

   Cost/Unit $_____ No. of Units _____ Total $_____

Notes: _____

_____

EXTRA NOTES

(Use tick marks at top & bottom to make graph paper)

BATHROOM NUMBER 3

FLOOR COVERING

Floor Measurements

Widest part of room from middle of doorway _____

Longest part of room from middle of doorway _____

Notes: _____

_____

Type & Material (nylon carpet, ceramic tile, etc.) _____

Purchased From _____ Date _____

Brand & Pattern _____

Color & No. _____ Warranty Period _____

Type of Backing _____ Pad Type _____

Cost/Unit $_____ No. of Units _____ Total $_____

Installed By _____ Attached With _____

Date _____ Cost $_____

Cleaned/Refinished By _____

Date 1 _____ Cost $_____

Date 2 _____ Cost $_____

Date 3 _____ Cost $_____

Notes: _____

CEILING COVERING

Type of Covering (paint, spray texture, etc.) _____

Purchased From _____ Date _____

Brand & Pattern _____

Color & No. _____ Warranty Period _____

Applied with (texture roller, sprayer, etc.) _____

Cost/Unit $_____ No. of Units _____ Total $_____

Installed By _____

Date _____ Cost $_____

Notes: _____

_____

22

WINDOW COVERING

Window 1 Measurements

Height _____ Width _____ Top of Window to Floor _____ Trim Width _____

Type of Covering (draperies, blinds, etc.) _____

Purchased From _____ Cost $_____ Date _____

    Measurements of Window Covering _____

    Material & Cleaning Instructions _____

Cleaned By _____ Cost $_____ Date _____

Cleaned By _____ Cost $_____ Date _____

Notes: _____

_____

Window 2 Measurements

Height _____ Width _____ Top of Window to Floor _____ Trim Width _____

Type of Covering (draperies, blinds, etc.) _____

Purchased From _____ Cost $_____ Date _____

    Measurements of Window Covering _____

    Material & Cleaning Instructions _____

Cleaned By _____ Cost $_____ Date _____

Notes: _____

WALL COVERING

Wall Measurements

    North _____ South _____ East _____ West _____

Use "2nd Type of Covering" for woodwork or paneling. It has a "Refinished By" section.

1ˢᵗ Type of Covering (paint, paper, etc.) _____

Purchased From _____ Date _____

    Brand & Pattern _____

    Color & No. _____ Warranty Period _____

    Cost/Unit $_____ No. of Units _____ Total $_____

Installed By _____

    Date _____ Cost $_____

Notes: _____

_____

WALL COVERING (continued)

2nd **Type of Covering** (woodwork, paneling, etc.) _____

Purchased From _____ Date _____

  Brand & Pattern _____

    Color & No. _____ Warranty Period _____

    Cost/Unit $_____ No. of Units _____ Total $_____

Installed By _____

  Date _____ Cost $_____

Refinished By _____

  Date _____ Cost $_____

Notes: _____

SAMPLES: PAINT, WALLPAPER, ETC.

attach swatch or paint daub here

FURNITURE/FIXTURES

Item	Purchased From	Date	Cost	Warranty

24

DOORS/TRIM

Purchased From _____ Date _____

    Brand & Style _____ Material (oak, steel, etc.)_____

    Stain/Paint Color & No. _____

      Finished With (polyurethane over stain, etc.) _____

Installed By _____ Total Cost $_____

Refinished By _____

    Refinished With _____

    Date _____ Cost $_____

Hardware Description _____

_____

    Purchased From _____ Date _____

    Cost/Unit $_____ No. of Units _____ Total $_____

Notes: _____

_____

EXTRA NOTES

(Use tick marks at top & bottom to make graph paper)

BEDROOM NUMBER I

FLOOR COVERING

Floor Measurements

Widest part of room from middle of doorway _____

Longest part of room from middle of doorway _____

Notes: _____

_____

Type & Material (nylon carpet, ceramic tile, etc.) _____

Purchased From _____ Date _____

Brand & Pattern _____

Color & No. _____ Warranty Period _____

Type of Backing _____ Pad Type _____

Cost/Unit $_____ No. of Units _____ Total $_____

Installed By _____ Attached With _____

Date _____ Cost $_____

Cleaned/Refinished By _____

Date 1 _____ Cost $_____

Date 2 _____ Cost $_____

Date 3 _____ Cost $_____

Notes: _____

CEILING COVERING

Type of Covering (paint, spray texture, etc.) _____

Purchased From _____ Date _____

Brand & Pattern _____

Color & No. _____ Warranty Period _____

Applied with (texture roller, sprayer, etc.) _____

Cost/Unit $_____ No. of Units _____ Total $_____

Installed By _____

Date _____ Cost $_____

Notes: _____

26

WINDOW COVERING

Window 1 Measurements

Height _____ Width _____ Top of Window to Floor _____ Trim Width _____

Type of Covering (draperies, blinds, etc.) _____

Purchased From _____ Cost $_____ Date _____

    Measurements of Window Covering _____

    Material & Cleaning Instructions _____

Cleaned By _____ Cost $_____ Date _____

Cleaned By _____ Cost $_____ Date _____

Notes: _____

_____

_____

Window 2 Measurements

Height _____ Width _____ Top of Window to Floor _____ Trim Width _____

Type of Covering (draperies, blinds, etc.) _____

Purchased From _____ Cost $_____ Date _____

    Measurements of Window Covering _____

    Material & Cleaning Instructions _____

Cleaned By _____ Cost $_____ Date _____

Notes: _____

_____

Window 3 Measurements

Height _____ Width _____ Top of Window to Floor _____ Trim Width _____

Type of Covering (draperies, blinds, etc.) _____

Purchased From _____ Cost $_____ Date _____

    Measurements of Window Covering _____

    Material & Cleaning Instructions _____

Cleaned By _____ Cost $_____ Date _____

Notes: _____

_____

WALL COVERING

Wall Measurements

North _____ South _____ East _____ West _____

Use "2nd Type of Covering" for woodwork or paneling. It has a "Refinished By" section.

1st Type of Covering (paint, paper, etc.) _____

Purchased From _____ Date _____

Brand & Pattern _____

Color & No. _____ Warranty Period _____

Cost/Unit $_____ No. of Units _____ Total $_____

Installed By _____

Date _____ Cost $_____

Notes: _____

_____

2nd Type of Covering (woodwork, paneling, etc.) _____

Purchased From _____ Date _____

Brand & Pattern _____

Color & No. _____ Warranty Period _____

Cost/Unit $_____ No. of Units _____ Total $_____

Installed By _____

Date _____ Cost $_____

Refinished By _____

Date _____ Cost $_____

Notes: _____

_____

SAMPLES: PAINT, WALLPAPER, ETC.

attach swatch or paint daub here

DOORS/TRIM

Purchased From _____ Date _____

    Brand & Style _____ Material (oak, steel, etc.)_____

    Stain/Paint Color & No. _____

    Finished With (polyurethane over stain, etc.) _____

Installed By _____ Total Cost $_____

Refinished By _____

    Refinished With _____

    Date _____ Cost $_____

Hardware Description _____

_____

    Purchased From _____ Date _____

    Cost/Unit $_____ No. of Units _____ Total $_____

Notes: _____

_____

FURNITURE/FIXTURES

Item	Purchased From	Date	Cost	Warranty

EXTRA NOTES

(Use tick marks at top & bottom to make graph paper)

29

BEDROOM NUMBER 2

FLOOR COVERING

Floor Measurements

Widest part of room from middle of doorway _____

Longest part of room from middle of doorway _____

Notes: _____

_____

Type & Material (nylon carpet, ceramic tile, etc.) _____

Purchased From _____ Date _____

Brand & Pattern _____

Color & No. _____ Warranty Period _____

Type of Backing _____ Pad Type _____

Cost/Unit $_____ No. of Units _____ Total $_____

Installed By _____ Attached With _____

Date _____ Cost $_____

Cleaned/Refinished By _____

Date 1 _____ Cost $_____

Date 2 _____ Cost $_____

Date 3 _____ Cost $_____

Notes: _____

_____

CEILING COVERING

Type of Covering (paint, spray texture, etc.) _____

Purchased From _____ Date _____

Brand & Pattern _____

Color & No. _____ Warranty Period _____

Applied with (texture roller, sprayer, etc.) _____

Cost/Unit $_____ No. of Units _____ Total $_____

Installed By _____

Date _____ Cost $_____

Notes: _____

_____

WINDOW COVERING

Window 1 Measurements

Height _____ Width _____ Top of Window to Floor _____ Trim Width _____

Type of Covering (draperies, blinds, etc.) _____

Purchased From _____ Cost $_____ Date _____

   Measurements of Window Covering _____

   Material & Cleaning Instructions _____

Cleaned By _____ Cost $_____ Date _____

Cleaned By _____ Cost $_____ Date _____

Notes: _____

_____

_____

Window 2 Measurements

Height _____ Width _____ Top of Window to Floor _____ Trim Width _____

Type of Covering (draperies, blinds, etc.) _____

Purchased From _____ Cost $_____ Date _____

   Measurements of Window Covering _____

   Material & Cleaning Instructions _____

Cleaned By _____ Cost $_____ Date _____

Notes: _____

_____

Window 3 Measurements

Height _____ Width _____ Top of Window to Floor _____ Trim Width _____

Type of Covering (draperies, blinds, etc.) _____

Purchased From _____ Cost $_____ Date _____

   Measurements of Window Covering _____

   Material & Cleaning Instructions _____

Cleaned By _____ Cost $_____ Date _____

Notes: _____

_____

WALL COVERING

<u>**Wall Measurements**</u>

North _____ South _____ East _____ West _____

Use "2nd Type of Covering" for woodwork or paneling. It has a "Refinished By" section.

1st Type of Covering (paint, paper, etc.) _____

Purchased From _____ Date _____

    Brand & Pattern _____

    Color & No. _____ Warranty Period _____

    Cost/Unit $_____ No. of Units _____ Total $_____

Installed By _____

    Date _____ Cost $_____

Notes: _____

_____

2nd Type of Covering (paint, paper, etc.) _____

Purchased From _____ Date _____

    Brand & Pattern _____

    Color & No. _____ Warranty Period _____

    Cost/Unit $_____ No. of Units _____ Total $_____

Installed By _____

    Date _____ Cost $_____

Refinished By _____

    Date _____ Cost $_____

Notes: _____

_____

SAMPLES: PAINT, WALLPAPER, ETC.

attach swatch or paint daub here

32

DOORS/TRIM

Purchased From _____ Date _____

    Brand & Style _____ Material (oak, steel, etc.)_____

    Stain/Paint Color & No. _____

        Finished With (polyurethane over stain, etc.) _____

Installed By _____ Total Cost $_____

Refinished By _____

    Refinished With _____

    Date _____ Cost $_____

Hardware Description _____

_____

    Purchased From _____ Date _____

    Cost/Unit $_____ No. of Units _____ Total $_____

Notes: _____

_____

FURNITURE/FIXTURES

Item	Purchased From	Date	Cost	Warranty

EXTRA NOTES
(Use tick marks at top & bottom to make graph paper)

33

BEDROOM NUMBER 3

FLOOR COVERING

Floor Measurements

Widest part of room from middle of doorway _____

Longest part of room from middle of doorway _____

Notes: _____

_____

Type & Material (nylon carpet, ceramic tile, etc.) _____

Purchased From _____ Date _____

Brand & Pattern _____

Color & No. _____ Warranty Period _____

Type of Backing _____ Pad Type _____

Cost/Unit $_____ No. of Units _____ Total $_____

Installed By _____ Attached With _____

Date _____ Cost $_____

Cleaned/Refinished By _____

Date 1 _____ Cost $_____

Date 2 _____ Cost $_____

Date 3 _____ Cost $_____

Notes: _____

CEILING COVERING

Type of Covering (paint, spray texture, etc.) _____

Purchased From _____ Date _____

Brand & Pattern _____

Color & No. _____ Warranty Period _____

Applied with (texture roller, sprayer, etc.) _____

Cost/Unit $_____ No. of Units _____ Total $_____

Installed By _____

Date _____ Cost $_____

Notes: _____

34

WINDOW COVERING

Window 1 Measurements

Height _____ Width _____ Top of Window to Floor _____ Trim Width _____

Type of Covering (draperies, blinds, etc.) _____

Purchased From _____ Cost $_____ Date _____

   Measurements of Window Covering _____

   Material & Cleaning Instructions _____

Cleaned By _____ Cost $_____ Date _____

Cleaned By _____ Cost $_____ Date _____

Notes: _____

_____

_____

Window 2 Measurements

Height _____ Width _____ Top of Window to Floor _____ Trim Width _____

Type of Covering (draperies, blinds, etc.) _____

Purchased From _____ Cost $_____ Date _____

   Measurements of Window Covering _____

   Material & Cleaning Instructions _____

Cleaned By _____ Cost $_____ Date _____

Notes: _____

_____

Window 3 Measurements

Height _____ Width _____ Top of Window to Floor _____ Trim Width _____

Type of Covering (draperies, blinds, etc.) _____

Purchased From _____ Cost $_____ Date _____

   Measurements of Window Covering _____

   Material & Cleaning Instructions _____

Cleaned By _____ Cost $_____ Date _____

Notes: _____

_____

35

WALL COVERING

Wall Measurements

North _____ South _____ East _____ West _____

Use "2nd Type of Covering" for woodwork or paneling. It has a "Refinished By" section.

1ˢᵗ Type of Covering (paint, paper, etc.) _____

Purchased From _____ Date _____

Brand & Pattern _____

Color & No. _____ Warranty Period _____

Cost/Unit $_____ No. of Units _____ Total $_____

Installed By _____

Date _____ Cost $_____

Notes: _____

_____

2ⁿᵈ Type of Covering (woodwork, paneling, etc.) _____

Purchased From _____ Date _____

Brand & Pattern _____

Color & No. _____ Warranty Period _____

Cost/Unit $_____ No. of Units _____ Total $_____

Installed By _____

Date _____ Cost $_____

Refinished By _____

Date _____ Cost $_____

Notes: _____

_____

SAMPLES: PAINT, WALLPAPER, ETC.

attach swatch or paint daub here

36

DOORS/TRIM

Purchased From _____ Date _____

  Brand & Style _____ Material (oak, steel, etc.)_____

  Stain/Paint Color & No. _____

    Finished With (polyurethane over stain, etc.) _____

Installed By _____ Total Cost $_____

Refinished By _____

  Refinished With _____

  Date _____ Cost $_____

Hardware Description _____

_____

  Purchased From _____ Date _____

  Cost/Unit $_____ No. of Units _____ Total $_____

Notes: _____

_____

FURNITURE/FIXTURES

Item	Purchased From	Date	Cost	Warranty

EXTRA NOTES
(Use tick marks at top & bottom to make graph paper)

37

BEDROOM NUMBER 4

FLOOR COVERING

Floor Measurements

Widest part of room from middle of doorway _____

Longest part of room from middle of doorway _____

Notes: _____

_____

Type & Material (nylon carpet, ceramic tile, etc.) _____

Purchased From _____ Date _____

Brand & Pattern _____

Color & No. _____ Warranty Period _____

Type of Backing _____ Pad Type _____

Cost/Unit $_____ No. of Units _____ Total $_____

Installed By _____ Attached With _____

Date _____ Cost $_____

Cleaned/Refinished By _____

Date 1 _____ Cost $_____

Date 2 _____ Cost $_____

Date 3 _____ Cost $_____

Notes: _____

_____

CEILING COVERING

Type of Covering (paint, spray texture, etc.) _____

Purchased From _____ Date _____

Brand & Pattern _____

Color & No. _____ Warranty Period _____

Applied with (texture roller, sprayer, etc.) _____

Cost/Unit $_____ No. of Units _____ Total $_____

Installed By _____

Date _____ Cost $_____

Notes: _____

_____

WINDOW COVERING

Window 1 Measurements

Height _____ Width _____ Top of Window to Floor _____ Trim Width _____

Type of Covering (draperies, blinds, etc.) _____

Purchased From _____ Cost $_____ Date _____

    Measurements of Window Covering _____

    Material & Cleaning Instructions _____

Cleaned By _____ Cost $_____ Date _____

Cleaned By _____ Cost $_____ Date _____

Notes: _____

_____

_____

Window 2 Measurements

Height _____ Width _____ Top of Window to Floor _____ Trim Width _____

Type of Covering (draperies, blinds, etc.) _____

Purchased From _____ Cost $_____ Date _____

    Measurements of Window Covering _____

    Material & Cleaning Instructions _____

Cleaned By _____ Cost $_____ Date _____

Notes: _____

_____

Window 3 Measurements

Height _____ Width _____ Top of Window to Floor _____ Trim Width _____

Type of Covering (draperies, blinds, etc.) _____

Purchased From _____ Cost $_____ Date _____

    Measurements of Window Covering _____

    Material & Cleaning Instructions _____

Cleaned By _____ Cost $_____ Date _____

Notes: _____

_____

WALL COVERING

<u>Wall Measurements</u>

North _____ South _____ East _____ West _____

Use "2nd Type of Covering" for woodwork or paneling. It has a "Refinished By" section.

1st Type of Covering (paint, paper, etc.) _____

Purchased From _____ Date _____

    Brand & Pattern _____

    Color & No. _____ Warranty Period _____

    Cost/Unit $_____ No. of Units _____ Total $_____

Installed By _____

    Date _____ Cost $_____

Notes: _____

_____

2nd Type of Covering (woodwork, paneling, etc.) _____

Purchased From _____ Date _____

    Brand & Pattern _____

    Color & No. _____ Warranty Period _____

    Cost/Unit $_____ No. of Units _____ Total $_____

Installed By _____

    Date _____ Cost $_____

Refinished By _____

    Date _____ Cost $_____

Notes: _____

_____

SAMPLES: PAINT, WALLPAPER, ETC.

attach swatch or paint daub here

DOORS/TRIM

Purchased From _____ Date _____

Brand & Style _____ Material (oak, steel, etc.)_____

Stain/Paint Color & No. _____

Finished With (polyurethane over stain, etc.) _____

Installed By _____ Total Cost $_____

Refinished By _____

Refinished With _____

Date _____ Cost $_____

Hardware Description _____

_____

Purchased From _____ Date _____

Cost/Unit $_____ No. of Units _____ Total $_____

Notes: _____

FURNITURE/FIXTURES

Item	Purchased From	Date	Cost	Warranty

EXTRA NOTES
(Use tick marks at top & bottom to make graph paper)

41

DEN/STUDY/OFFICE

FLOOR COVERING

Floor Measurements

Widest part of room from middle of doorway _____

Longest part of room from middle of doorway _____

Notes: _____

_____

Type & Material (nylon carpet, ceramic tile, etc.) _____

Purchased From _____ Date _____

Brand & Pattern _____

Color & No. _____ Warranty Period _____

Type of Backing _____ Pad Type _____

Cost/Unit $_____ No. of Units _____ Total $_____

Installed By _____ Attached With _____

Date _____ Cost $_____

Cleaned/Refinished By _____

Date 1 _____ Cost $_____

Date 2 _____ Cost $_____

Date 3 _____ Cost $_____

Notes: _____

CEILING COVERING

Type of Covering (paint, spray texture, etc.) _____

Purchased From _____ Date _____

Brand & Pattern _____

Color & No. _____ Warranty Period _____

Applied with (texture roller, sprayer, etc.) _____

Cost/Unit $_____ No. of Units _____ Total $_____

Installed By _____

Date _____ Cost $_____

Notes: _____

_____

DEN/STUDY/OFFICE (continued)

WINDOW COVERING

Window 1 Measurements

Height _____ Width _____ Top of Window to Floor _____ Trim Width _____

Type of Covering (draperies, blinds, etc.) _____

Purchased From _____ Cost $_____ Date _____

   Measurements of Window Covering _____

   Material & Cleaning Instructions _____

Cleaned By _____ Cost $_____ Date _____

Cleaned By _____ Cost $_____ Date _____

Notes: _____

_____

_____

Window 2 Measurements

Height _____ Width _____ Top of Window to Floor _____ Trim Width _____

Type of Covering (draperies, blinds, etc.) _____

Purchased From _____ Cost $_____ Date _____

   Measurements of Window Covering _____

   Material & Cleaning Instructions _____

Cleaned By _____ Cost $_____ Date _____

Notes: _____

_____

Window 3 Measurements

Height _____ Width _____ Top of Window to Floor _____ Trim Width _____

Type of Covering (draperies, blinds, etc.) _____

Purchased From _____ Cost $_____ Date _____

   Measurements of Window Covering _____

   Material & Cleaning Instructions _____

Cleaned By _____ Cost $_____ Date _____

Notes: _____

_____

WALL COVERING
Wall Measurements

North _____ South _____ East _____ West _____

Use "2nd Type of Covering" for woodwork or paneling. It has a "Refinished By" section.

1ˢᵗ Type of Covering (paint, paper, etc.) _____

Purchased From _____ Date _____

   Brand & Pattern _____

   Color & No. _____ Warranty Period _____

   Cost/Unit $_____ No. of Units _____ Total $_____

Installed By _____

   Date _____ Cost $_____

Notes: _____

_____

2ⁿᵈ Type of Covering (woodwork, paneling, etc.) _____

Purchased From _____ Date _____

   Brand & Pattern _____

   Color & No. _____ Warranty Period _____

   Cost/Unit $_____ No. of Units _____ Total $_____

Installed By _____

   Date _____ Cost $_____

Refinished By _____

   Date _____ Cost $_____

Notes: _____

_____

SAMPLES: PAINT, WALLPAPER, ETC.

attach swatch or paint daub here

44

DOORS/TRIM

Purchased From _____ Date _____

   Brand & Style _____ Material (oak, steel, etc.)_____

   Stain/Paint Color & No. _____

     Finished With (polyurethane over stain, etc.) _____

Installed By _____ Total Cost $_____

Refinished By _____

   Refinished With _____

   Date _____ Cost $_____

Hardware Description _____

_____

   Purchased From _____ Date _____

   Cost/Unit $_____ No. of Units _____ Total $_____

Notes: _____

_____

FURNITURE/FIXTURES

Item	Purchased From	Date	Cost	Warranty

EXTRA NOTES
(Use tick marks at top & bottom to make graph paper)

45

DINING ROOM

FLOOR COVERING

Floor Measurements

Widest part of room from middle of doorway _____

Longest part of room from middle of doorway _____

Notes: _____

_____

Type & Material (nylon carpet, ceramic tile, etc.) _____

Purchased From _____ Date _____

Brand & Pattern _____

Color & No. _____ Warranty Period _____

Type of Backing _____ Pad Type _____

Cost/Unit $_____ No. of Units _____ Total $_____

Installed By _____ Attached With _____

Date _____ Cost $_____

Cleaned/Refinished By _____

Date 1 _____ Cost $_____

Date 2 _____ Cost $_____

Date 3 _____ Cost $_____

Notes: _____

_____

CEILING COVERING

Type of Covering (paint, spray texture, etc.) _____

Purchased From _____ Date _____

Brand & Pattern _____

Color & No. _____ Warranty Period _____

Applied with (texture roller, sprayer, etc.) _____

Cost/Unit $_____ No. of Units _____ Total $_____

Installed By _____

Date _____ Cost $_____

Notes: _____

_____

WINDOW COVERING

Window 1 Measurements

Height _____ Width _____ Top of Window to Floor _____ Trim Width _____

Type of Covering (draperies, blinds, etc.) _____

Purchased From _____ Cost $_____ Date _____

Measurements of Window Covering _____

Material & Cleaning Instructions _____

Cleaned By _____ Cost $_____ Date _____

Cleaned By _____ Cost $_____ Date _____

Notes: _____

_____

_____

Window 2 Measurements

Height _____ Width _____ Top of Window to Floor _____ Trim Width _____

Type of Covering (draperies, blinds, etc.) _____

Purchased From _____ Cost $_____ Date _____

Measurements of Window Covering _____

Material & Cleaning Instructions _____

Cleaned By _____ Cost $_____ Date _____

Notes: _____

_____

Window 3 Measurements

Height _____ Width _____ Top of Window to Floor _____ Trim Width _____

Type of Covering (draperies, blinds, etc.) _____

Purchased From _____ Cost $_____ Date _____

Measurements of Window Covering _____

Material & Cleaning Instructions _____

Cleaned By _____ Cost $_____ Date _____

Notes: _____

_____

47

WALL COVERING
Wall Measurements

North _____ South _____ East _____ West _____

Use "2nd Type of Covering" for woodwork or paneling. It has a "Refinished By" section.

1ˢᵗ Type of Covering (paint, paper, etc.) _____

Purchased From _____ Date _____

    Brand & Pattern _____

    Color & No. _____ Warranty Period _____

    Cost/Unit $_____ No. of Units _____ Total $_____

Installed By _____

    Date _____ Cost $_____

Notes: _____

_____

2ⁿᵈ Type of Covering (woodwork, paneling, etc.) _____

Purchased From _____ Date _____

    Brand & Pattern _____

    Color & No. _____ Warranty Period _____

    Cost/Unit $_____ No. of Units _____ Total $_____

Installed By _____

    Date _____ Cost $_____

Refinished By _____

    Date _____ Cost $_____

Notes: _____

_____

SAMPLES: PAINT, WALLPAPER, ETC.

attach swatch or paint daub here

48

DOORS/TRIM

Purchased From _____ Date _____

   Brand & Style _____ Material (oak, steel, etc.)_____

   Stain/Paint Color & No. _____

    Finished With (polyurethane over stain, etc.) _____

Installed By _____ Total Cost $_____

Refinished By _____

   Refinished With _____

   Date _____ Cost $_____

Hardware Description _____

_____

   Purchased From _____ Date _____

   Cost/Unit $_____ No. of Units _____ Total $_____

Notes: _____

_____

FURNITURE/FIXTURES

Item	Purchased From	Date	Cost	Warranty

EXTRA NOTES
(Use tick marks at top & bottom to make graph paper)

49

ELECTRICAL/WIRING

(Suggestion: Use tick marks at top & bottom to make graph paper. Sketch the layout of your circuit/fuse box. Label the circuits/fuses and identify the outlets and appliances they control.)

ENTRY/FOYER/MUD ROOM

FLOOR COVERING

Floor Measurements

Widest part of room from middle of doorway _____

Longest part of room from middle of doorway _____

Notes: _____

_____

Type & Material (nylon carpet, ceramic tile, etc.) _____

Purchased From _____ Date _____

Brand & Pattern _____

Color & No. _____ Warranty Period _____

Type of Backing _____ Pad Type _____

Cost/Unit $_____ No. of Units _____ Total $_____

Installed By _____ Attached With _____

Date _____ Cost $_____

Cleaned/Refinished By _____

Date 1 _____ Cost $_____

Date 2 _____ Cost $_____

Date 3 _____ Cost $_____

Notes: _____

_____

CEILING COVERING

Type of Covering (paint, spray texture, etc.) _____

Purchased From _____ Date _____

Brand & Pattern _____

Color & No. _____ Warranty Period _____

Applied with (texture roller, sprayer, etc.) _____

Cost/Unit $_____ No. of Units _____ Total $_____

Installed By _____

Date _____ Cost $_____

Notes: _____

_____

WINDOW COVERING

Window Measurements

Height _____ Width _____ Top of Window to Floor _____ Trim Width _____

Type of Covering (draperies, blinds, etc.) _____

Purchased From _____ Cost $_____ Date _____

   Measurements of Window Covering _____

   Material & Cleaning Instructions _____

Cleaned By _____ Cost $_____ Date ____

Cleaned By _____ Cost $_____ Date ____

Notes: _____

WALL COVERING

Wall Measurements

   North _____ South _____ East _____ West _____

   Use "2nd Type of Covering" for woodwork or paneling. It has a "Refinished By" section.

1st Type of Covering (paint, paper, etc.) _____

Purchased From _____ Date _____

   Brand & Pattern _____

   Color & No. _____ Warranty Period _____

   Cost/Unit $_____ No. of Units _____ Total $_____

Installed By _____

   Date _____ Cost $_____

Notes: _____

2nd Type of Covering (woodwork, paneling, etc.) _____

Purchased From _____ Date _____

   Brand & Pattern _____

   Color & No. _____ Warranty Period _____

   Cost/Unit $_____ No. of Units _____ Total $_____

Installed By _____

   Date _____ Cost $_____

Refinished By _____

   Date _____ Cost $_____

Notes: _____

SAMPLES: PAINT, WALLPAPER, ETC.

attach swatch or paint daub here

DOORS/TRIM

Purchased From _____ Date _____

Brand & Style _____ Material (oak, steel, etc.)_____

Stain/Paint Color & No. _____

Finished With (polyurethane over stain, etc.) _____

Installed By _____ Total Cost $_____

Refinished By _____

Refinished With _____

Date _____ Cost $_____

Hardware Description _____

Purchased From _____ Date _____

Cost/Unit $_____ No. of Units _____ Total $_____

Notes: _____

FURNITURE/FIXTURES

Item	Purchased From	Date	Cost	Warranty

EXTRA NOTES

FAMILY ROOM

FLOOR COVERING

Floor Measurements

Widest part of room from middle of doorway _____

Longest part of room from middle of doorway _____

Notes: _____

_____

Type & Material (nylon carpet, ceramic tile, etc.) _____

Purchased From _____ Date _____

Brand & Pattern _____

Color & No. _____ Warranty Period _____

Type of Backing _____ Pad Type _____

Cost/Unit $_____ No. of Units _____ Total $_____

Installed By _____ Attached With _____

Date _____ Cost $_____

Cleaned/Refinished By _____

Date 1 _____ Cost $_____

Date 2 _____ Cost $_____

Date 3 _____ Cost $_____

Notes: _____

_____

CEILING COVERING

Type of Covering (paint, spray texture, etc.) _____

Purchased From _____ Date _____

Brand & Pattern _____

Color & No. _____ Warranty Period _____

Applied with (texture roller, sprayer, etc.) _____

Cost/Unit $_____ No. of Units _____ Total $_____

Installed By _____

Date _____ Cost $_____

Notes: _____

_____

WINDOW COVERING

Window 1 Measurements

Height _____ Width _____ Top of Window to Floor _____ Trim Width _____

Type of Covering (draperies, blinds, etc.) _____

Purchased From _____ Cost $_____ Date _____

   Measurements of Window Covering _____

   Material & Cleaning Instructions _____

Cleaned By _____ Cost $_____ Date _____

Cleaned By _____ Cost $_____ Date _____

Notes: _____

_____

_____

Window 2 Measurements

Height _____ Width _____ Top of Window to Floor _____ Trim Width _____

Type of Covering (draperies, blinds, etc.) _____

Purchased From _____ Cost $_____ Date _____

   Measurements of Window Covering _____

   Material & Cleaning Instructions _____

Cleaned By _____ Cost $_____ Date _____

Notes: _____

_____

Window 3 Measurements

Height _____ Width _____ Top of Window to Floor _____ Trim Width _____

Type of Covering (draperies, blinds, etc.) _____

Purchased From _____ Cost $_____ Date _____

   Measurements of Window Covering _____

   Material & Cleaning Instructions _____

Cleaned By _____ Cost $_____ Date _____

Notes: _____

_____

WALL COVERING

Wall Measurements

North _____ South _____ East _____ West _____

Use "2nd Type of Covering" for woodwork or paneling. It has a "Refinished By" section.

1st Type of Covering (paint, paper, etc.) _____

Purchased From _____ Date _____

Brand & Pattern _____

Color & No. _____ Warranty Period _____

Cost/Unit $_____ No. of Units _____ Total $_____

Installed By _____

Date _____ Cost $_____

Notes: _____

_____

2nd Type of Covering (woodwork, paneling, etc.) _____

Purchased From _____ Date _____

Brand & Pattern _____

Color & No. _____ Warranty Period _____

Cost/Unit $_____ No. of Units _____ Total $_____

Installed By _____

Date _____ Cost $_____

Refinished By _____

Date _____ Cost $_____

Notes: _____

_____

SAMPLES: PAINT, WALLPAPER, ETC.

attach swatch or paint daub here

FAMILY ROOM (continued)

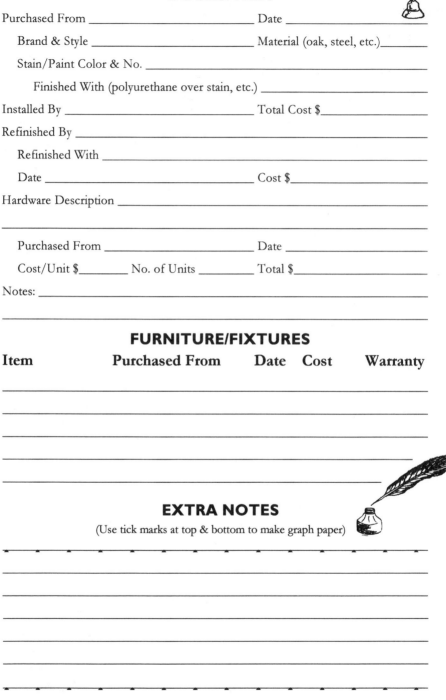

DOORS/TRIM

Purchased From _____ Date _____

    Brand & Style _____ Material (oak, steel, etc.)_____

    Stain/Paint Color & No. _____

       Finished With (polyurethane over stain, etc.) _____

Installed By _____ Total Cost $_____

Refinished By _____

    Refinished With _____

    Date _____ Cost $_____

Hardware Description _____

_____

    Purchased From _____ Date _____

    Cost/Unit $_____ No. of Units _____ Total $_____

Notes: _____

FURNITURE/FIXTURES

Item	Purchased From	Date	Cost	Warranty

EXTRA NOTES
(Use tick marks at top & bottom to make graph paper)

HALLWAY/STAIRWAY I

FLOOR COVERING

Floor Measurements

Widest part of room from middle of doorway _____

Longest part of room from middle of doorway _____

Notes: _____

_____

Type & Material (nylon carpet, ceramic tile, etc.) _____

Purchased From _____ Date _____

    Brand & Pattern _____

    Color & No. _____ Warranty Period _____

    Type of Backing _____ Pad Type _____

    Cost/Unit $_____ No. of Units _____ Total $_____

Installed By _____ Attached With _____

    Date _____ Cost $_____

Cleaned/Refinished By _____

    Date 1 _____ Cost $_____

    Date 2 _____ Cost $_____

    Date 3 _____ Cost $_____

Notes: _____

_____

CEILING COVERING

Type of Covering (paint, spray texture, etc.) _____

Purchased From _____ Date _____

    Brand & Pattern _____

    Color & No. _____ Warranty Period _____

    Applied with (texture roller, sprayer, etc.) _____

    Cost/Unit $_____ No. of Units _____ Total $_____

Installed By _____

    Date _____ Cost $_____

Notes: _____

_____

WINDOW COVERING

Window Measurements

Height _____ Width _____ Top of Window to Floor _____ Trim Width _____

Type of Covering (draperies, blinds, etc.) _____

Purchased From _____ Cost $_____ Date _____

    Measurements of Window Covering _____

    Material & Cleaning Instructions _____

Cleaned By _____ Cost $_____ Date _____

Cleaned By _____ Cost $_____ Date _____

Notes: _____

WALL COVERING

Wall Measurements

    North _____ South _____ East _____ West _____

    Use "2nd Type of Covering" for woodwork or paneling. It has a "Refinished By" section.

1ˢᵗ Type of Covering (paint, paper, etc.) _____

Purchased From _____ Date _____

    Brand & Pattern _____

    Color & No. _____ Warranty Period _____

    Cost/Unit $_____ No. of Units _____ Total $_____

Installed By _____

    Date _____ Cost $_____

Notes: _____

2ⁿᵈ Type of Covering (woodwork, paneling, etc.) _____

Purchased From _____ Date _____

    Brand & Pattern _____

    Color & No. _____ Warranty Period _____

    Cost/Unit $_____ No. of Units _____ Total $_____

Installed By _____

    Date _____ Cost $_____

Refinished By _____

    Date _____ Cost $_____

Notes: _____

SAMPLES: PAINT, WALLPAPER, ETC.

attach swatch or paint daub here

DOORS/TRIM

Purchased From _____ Date _____

Brand & Style _____ Material (oak, steel, etc.)_____

Stain/Paint Color & No. _____

Finished With (polyurethane over stain, etc.) _____

Installed By _____ Total Cost $_____

Refinished By _____

Refinished With _____

Date _____ Cost $_____

Hardware Description _____

Purchased From _____ Date _____

Cost/Unit $_____ No. of Units _____ Total $_____

Notes: _____

FURNITURE/FIXTURES

Item	Purchased From	Date	Cost	Warranty

EXTRA NOTES

HALLWAY/STAIRWAY 2

FLOOR COVERING

Floor Measurements

Widest part of room from middle of doorway _____

Longest part of room from middle of doorway _____

Notes: _____

_____

Type & Material (nylon carpet, ceramic tile, etc.) _____

Purchased From _____ Date _____

Brand & Pattern _____

Color & No. _____ Warranty Period _____

Type of Backing _____ Pad Type _____

Cost/Unit $_____ No. of Units _____ Total $_____

Installed By _____ Attached With _____

Date _____ Cost $_____

Cleaned/Refinished By _____

Date 1 _____ Cost $_____

Date 2 _____ Cost $_____

Date 3 _____ Cost $_____

Notes: _____

CEILING COVERING

Type of Covering (paint, spray texture, etc.) _____

Purchased From _____ Date _____

Brand & Pattern _____

Color & No. _____ Warranty Period _____

Applied with (texture roller, sprayer, etc.) _____

Cost/Unit $_____ No. of Units _____ Total $_____

Installed By _____

Date _____ Cost $_____

Notes: _____

62

WINDOW COVERING

Window Measurements

Height _____ Width _____ Top of Window to Floor _____ Trim Width _____

Type of Covering (draperies, blinds, etc.) _____

Purchased From _____ Cost $_____ Date _____

    Measurements of Window Covering _____

    Material & Cleaning Instructions _____

Cleaned By _____ Cost $_____ Date _____

Cleaned By _____ Cost $_____ Date _____

Notes: _____

WALL COVERING

Wall Measurements

    North _____ South _____ East _____ West _____

    Use "2nd Type of Covering" for woodwork or paneling. It has a "Refinished By" section.

1st Type of Covering (paint, paper, etc.) _____

Purchased From _____ Date _____

    Brand & Pattern _____

    Color & No. _____ Warranty Period _____

    Cost/Unit $_____ No. of Units _____ Total $_____

Installed By _____

    Date _____ Cost $_____

Notes: _____

2nd Type of Covering (woodwork, paneling, etc.) _____

Purchased From _____ Date _____

    Brand & Pattern _____

    Color & No. _____ Warranty Period _____

    Cost/Unit $_____ No. of Units _____ Total $_____

Installed By _____

    Date _____ Cost $_____

Refinished By _____

    Date _____ Cost $_____

Notes: _____

SAMPLES: PAINT, WALLPAPER, ETC.

attach swatch or paint daub here

DOORS/TRIM

Purchased From _____ Date _____

    Brand & Style _____ Material (oak, steel, etc.)_____

    Stain/Paint Color & No. _____

        Finished With (polyurethane over stain, etc.) _____

Installed By _____ Total Cost $_____

Refinished By _____

    Refinished With _____

    Date _____ Cost $_____

Hardware Description _____

    Purchased From _____ Date _____

    Cost/Unit $_____ No. of Units _____ Total $_____

Notes: _____

FURNITURE/FIXTURES

Item	Purchased From	Date	Cost	Warranty

EXTRA NOTES

_____

_____

_____

_____

HALLWAY/STAIRWAY 3

FLOOR COVERING

Floor Measurements

Widest part of room from middle of doorway _____

Longest part of room from middle of doorway _____

Notes: _____

_____

Type & Material (nylon carpet, ceramic tile, etc.) _____

Purchased From _____ Date _____

    Brand & Pattern _____

    Color & No. _____ Warranty Period _____

    Type of Backing _____ Pad Type _____

    Cost/Unit $_____ No. of Units _____ Total $_____

Installed By _____ Attached With _____

    Date _____ Cost $_____

Cleaned/Refinished By _____

    Date 1 _____ Cost $_____

    Date 2 _____ Cost $_____

    Date 3 _____ Cost $_____

Notes: _____

_____

CEILING COVERING

Type of Covering (paint, spray texture, etc.) _____

Purchased From _____ Date _____

    Brand & Pattern _____

    Color & No. _____ Warranty Period _____

    Applied with (texture roller, sprayer, etc.) _____

    Cost/Unit $_____ No. of Units _____ Total $_____

Installed By _____

    Date _____ Cost $_____

Notes: _____

_____

WINDOW COVERING

Window Measurements

Height _____ Width _____ Top of Window to Floor _____ Trim Width _____

Type of Covering (draperies, blinds, etc.) _____

Purchased From _____ Cost $_____ Date _____

   Measurements of Window Covering _____

   Material & Cleaning Instructions _____

Cleaned By _____ Cost $_____ Date _____

Cleaned By _____ Cost $_____ Date _____

Notes: _____

WALL COVERING

Wall Measurements

   North _____ South _____ East _____ West _____

   Use "2nd Type of Covering" for woodwork or paneling. It has a "Refinished By" section.

1st **Type of Covering** (paint, paper, etc.) _____

Purchased From _____ Date _____

   Brand & Pattern _____

   Color & No. _____ Warranty Period _____

   Cost/Unit $_____ No. of Units _____ Total $_____

Installed By _____

   Date _____ Cost $_____

Notes: _____

2nd **Type of Covering** (woodwork, paneling, etc.) _____

Purchased From _____ Date _____

   Brand & Pattern _____

   Color & No. _____ Warranty Period _____

   Cost/Unit $_____ No. of Units _____ Total $_____

Installed By _____

   Date _____ Cost $_____

Refinished By _____

   Date _____ Cost $_____

Notes: _____

SAMPLES: PAINT, WALLPAPER, ETC.

attach swatch or paint daub here

DOORS/TRIM

Purchased From _____ Date _____

Brand & Style _____ Material (oak, steel, etc.)_____

Stain/Paint Color & No. _____

Finished With (polyurethane over stain, etc.) _____

Installed By _____ Total Cost $_____

Refinished By _____

Refinished With _____

Date _____ Cost $_____

Hardware Description _____

Purchased From _____ Date _____

Cost/Unit $_____ No. of Units _____ Total $_____

Notes: _____

FURNITURE/FIXTURES

Item	Purchased From	Date	Cost	Warranty

EXTRA NOTES

_____

_____

_____

_____

KITCHEN

FLOOR COVERING

Floor Measurements

Widest part of room from middle of doorway _____

Longest part of room from middle of doorway _____

Notes: _____

_____

Type & Material (nylon carpet, ceramic tile, etc.) _____

Purchased From _____ Date _____

Brand & Pattern _____

Color & No. _____ Warranty Period _____

Type of Backing _____ Pad Type _____

Cost/Unit $_____ No. of Units _____ Total $_____

Installed By _____ Attached With _____

Date _____ Cost $_____

Cleaned/Refinished By _____

Date 1 _____ Cost $_____

Date 2 _____ Cost $_____

Date 3 _____ Cost $_____

Notes: _____

CEILING COVERING

Type of Covering (paint, spray texture, etc.) _____

Purchased From _____ Date _____

Brand & Pattern _____

Color & No. _____ Warranty Period _____

Applied with (texture roller, sprayer, etc.) _____

Cost/Unit $_____ No. of Units _____ Total $_____

Installed By _____

Date _____ Cost $_____

Notes: _____

WINDOW COVERING

Window 1 Measurements

Height _____ Width _____ Top of Window to Floor _____ Trim Width _____

Type of Covering (draperies, blinds, etc.) _____

Purchased From _____ Cost $_____ Date _____

   Measurements of Window Covering _____

   Material & Cleaning Instructions _____

Cleaned By _____ Cost $_____ Date _____

Cleaned By _____ Cost $_____ Date _____

Notes: _____

_____

_____

Window 2 Measurements

Height _____ Width _____ Top of Window to Floor _____ Trim Width _____

Type of Covering (draperies, blinds, etc.) _____

Purchased From _____ Cost $_____ Date _____

   Measurements of Window Covering _____

   Material & Cleaning Instructions _____

Cleaned By _____ Cost $_____ Date _____

Notes: _____

_____

Window 3 Measurements

Height _____ Width _____ Top of Window to Floor _____ Trim Width _____

Type of Covering (draperies, blinds, etc.) _____

Purchased From _____ Cost $_____ Date _____

   Measurements of Window Covering _____

   Material & Cleaning Instructions _____

Cleaned By _____ Cost $_____ Date _____

Notes: _____

_____

WALL COVERING

Wall Measurements

North _____ South _____ East _____ West _____

Use "2nd Type of Covering" for woodwork or paneling. It has a "Refinished By" section.

1st Type of Covering (paint, paper, etc.) _____

Purchased From _____ Date _____

    Brand & Pattern _____

    Color & No. _____ Warranty Period _____

    Cost/Unit $_____ No. of Units _____ Total $_____

Installed By _____

    Date _____ Cost $_____

Notes: _____

_____

2nd Type of Covering (woodwork, paneling, etc.) _____

Purchased From _____ Date _____

    Brand & Pattern _____

    Color & No. _____ Warranty Period _____

    Cost/Unit $_____ No. of Units _____ Total $_____

Installed By _____

    Date _____ Cost $_____

Refinished By _____

    Date _____ Cost $_____

Notes: _____

_____

SAMPLES: PAINT, WALLPAPER, ETC.

attach swatch or paint daub here

CABINETS

Purchased From _____ Date _____

   Brand & Style _____ Material (oak, pine, etc.)_____

   Stain/Paint Color & No. _____

     Finished With (polyurethane over stain, etc.) _____

   Countertop Material _____

     Brand & Pattern _____ Color & No._____

Installed By _____ Total Cost $_____

Refinished By _____

   Refinished With _____

   Date _____ Cost $_____

Hardware Description _____

_____

   Purchased From _____ Date _____

   Cost/Unit $_____ No. of Units _____ Total $_____

Notes: _____

_____

DOORS/TRIM

Purchased From _____ Date _____

   Brand & Style _____ Material (oak, steel, etc.)_____

   Stain/Paint Color & No. _____

     Finished With (polyurethane over stain, etc.) _____

Installed By _____ Total Cost $_____

Refinished By _____

   Refinished With _____

   Date _____ Cost $_____

Hardware Description _____

_____

   Purchased From _____ Date _____

   Cost/Unit $_____ No. of Units _____ Total $_____

Notes: _____

MAJOR APPLIANCES

Type (range, dishwasher, etc.) _____ Manufacturer _____

Model/Lot No. _____ Serial No. _____

Purchased From _____ Cost _____ Date _____

Authorized Service Center _____ Warranty Period _____

Maintenance/Service _____

Notes: _____

Type (range, dishwasher, etc.) _____ Manufacturer _____

Model/Lot No. _____ Serial No. _____

Purchased From _____ Cost _____ Date _____

Authorized Service Center _____ Warranty Period _____

Maintenance/Service _____

Notes: _____

Type (range, dishwasher, etc.) _____ Manufacturer _____

Model/Lot No. _____ Serial No. _____

Purchased From _____ Cost _____ Date _____

Authorized Service Center _____ Warranty Period _____

Maintenance/Service _____

Notes: _____

Type (range, dishwasher, etc.) _____ Manufacturer _____

Model/Lot No. _____ Serial No. _____

Purchased From _____ Cost _____ Date _____

Authorized Service Center _____ Warranty Period _____

Maintenance/Service _____

Notes: _____

Type (range, dishwasher, etc.) _____ Manufacturer _____

Model/Lot No. _____ Serial No. _____

Purchased From _____ Cost _____ Date _____

Authorized Service Center _____ Warranty Period _____

Maintenance/Service _____

Notes: _____

FURNITURE/FIXTURES/SMALL APPLIANCES

Item	Purchased From	Date	Cost	Warranty

EXTRA NOTES

(Use tick marks at top & bottom to make graph paper)

LAUNDRY ROOM
FLOOR COVERING

Floor Measurements

Widest part of room from middle of doorway _____

Longest part of room from middle of doorway _____

Notes: _____

_____

Type & Material (linoleum, ceramic tile, etc.) _____

Purchased From _____ Date _____

    Brand & Pattern _____

    Color & No. _____ Warranty Period _____

    Type of Backing _____ Pad Type _____

    Cost/Unit $_____ No. of Units _____ Total $_____

Installed By _____ Attached With _____

    Date _____ Cost $_____

Cleaned/Refinished By _____

    Date 1 _____ Cost $_____

    Date 2 _____ Cost $_____

    Date 3 _____ Cost $_____

Notes: _____

_____

CEILING COVERING

Type of Covering (paint, spray texture, etc.) _____

Purchased From _____ Date _____

    Brand & Pattern _____

    Color & No. _____ Warranty Period _____

    Applied with (texture roller, sprayer, etc.) _____

    Cost/Unit $_____ No. of Units _____ Total $_____

Installed By _____

    Date _____ Cost $_____

Notes: _____

_____

WINDOW COVERING

Window Measurements

Height _____ Width _____ Top of Window to Floor _____ Trim Width _____

Type of Covering (draperies, blinds, etc.) _____

Purchased From _____ Cost $_____ Date _____

   Measurements of Window Covering _____

   Material & Cleaning Instructions _____

Cleaned By _____ Cost $_____ Date _____

Cleaned By _____ Cost $_____ Date _____

Notes: _____

WALL COVERING

Wall Measurements

   North _____ South _____ East _____ West _____

   Use "2nd Type of Covering" for woodwork or paneling. It has a "Refinished By" section.

1st Type of Covering (paint, paper, etc.) _____

Purchased From _____ Date _____

   Brand & Pattern _____

   Color & No. _____ Warranty Period _____

   Cost/Unit $_____ No. of Units _____ Total $_____

Installed By _____

   Date _____ Cost $_____

Notes: _____

2nd Type of Covering (woodwork, paneling, etc.) _____

Purchased From _____ Date _____

   Brand & Pattern _____

   Color & No. _____ Warranty Period _____

   Cost/Unit $_____ No. of Units _____ Total $_____

Installed By _____

   Date _____ Cost $_____

Refinished By _____

   Date _____ Cost $_____

Notes: _____

75

SAMPLES: PAINT, WALLPAPER, ETC.

attach swatch or paint daub here

MAJOR APPLIANCES

Type (washer, dryer, etc.) _____ Manufacturer _____

Model/Lot No. _____ Serial No. _____

Purchased From _____ Cost _____ Date _____

Authorized Service Center _____ Warranty Period _____

Maintenance/Service _____

Notes: _____

Type (washer, dryer, etc.) _____ Manufacturer _____

Model/Lot No. _____ Serial No. _____

Purchased From _____ Cost _____ Date _____

Authorized Service Center _____ Warranty Period _____

Maintenance/Service _____

Notes: _____

Type (washer, dryer, etc.) _____ Manufacturer _____

Model/Lot No. _____ Serial No. _____

Purchased From _____ Cost _____ Date _____

Authorized Service Center _____ Warranty Period _____

Maintenance/Service _____

Notes: _____

Type (washer, dryer, etc.) _____ Manufacturer _____

Model/Lot No. _____ Serial No. _____

Purchased From _____ Cost _____ Date _____

Authorized Service Center _____ Warranty Period _____

Maintenance/Service _____

Notes: _____

DOORS/TRIM

Purchased From _____ Date _____

    Brand & Style _____ Material (oak, steel, etc.)_____

    Stain/Paint Color & No. _____

       Finished With (polyurethane over stain, etc.) _____

Installed By _____ Total Cost $_____

Refinished By _____

    Refinished With _____

    Date _____ Cost $_____

Hardware Description _____

    Purchased From _____ Date _____

    Cost/Unit $_____ No. of Units _____ Total $_____

Notes: _____

FURNITURE/FIXTURES

Item	Purchased From	Date	Cost	Warranty

EXTRA NOTES

_____

_____

_____

_____

_____

_____

_____

_____

_____

LIVING ROOM

FLOOR COVERING

Floor Measurements

Widest part of room from middle of doorway _____

Longest part of room from middle of doorway _____

Notes: _____

_____

Type & Material (nylon carpet, ceramic tile, etc.) _____

Purchased From _____ Date _____

Brand & Pattern _____

Color & No. _____ Warranty Period _____

Type of Backing _____ Pad Type _____

Cost/Unit $_____ No. of Units _____ Total $_____

Installed By _____ Attached With _____

Date _____ Cost $_____

Cleaned/Refinished By _____

Date 1 _____ Cost $_____

Date 2 _____ Cost $_____

Date 3 _____ Cost $_____

Notes: _____

_____

CEILING COVERING

Type of Covering (paint, spray texture, etc.) _____

Purchased From _____ Date _____

Brand & Pattern _____

Color & No. _____ Warranty Period _____

Applied with (texture roller, sprayer, etc.) _____

Cost/Unit $_____ No. of Units _____ Total $_____

Installed By _____

Date _____ Cost $_____

Notes: _____

_____

78

WINDOW COVERING

Window 1 Measurements

Height _____ Width _____ Top of Window to Floor _____ Trim Width _____

Type of Covering (draperies, blinds, etc.) _____

Purchased From _____ Cost $_____ Date _____

    Measurements of Window Covering _____

    Material & Cleaning Instructions _____

Cleaned By _____ Cost $_____ Date _____

Cleaned By _____ Cost $_____ Date _____

Notes: _____

_____

_____

Window 2 Measurements

Height _____ Width _____ Top of Window to Floor _____ Trim Width _____

Type of Covering (draperies, blinds, etc.) _____

Purchased From _____ Cost $_____ Date _____

    Measurements of Window Covering _____

    Material & Cleaning Instructions _____

Cleaned By _____ Cost $_____ Date _____

Notes: _____

_____

Window 3 Measurements

Height _____ Width _____ Top of Window to Floor _____ Trim Width _____

Type of Covering (draperies, blinds, etc.) _____

Purchased From _____ Cost $_____ Date _____

    Measurements of Window Covering _____

    Material & Cleaning Instructions _____

Cleaned By _____ Cost $_____ Date _____

Notes: _____

_____

WALL COVERING

Wall Measurements

North _____ South _____ East _____ West _____

Use "2nd Type of Covering" for woodwork or paneling. It has a "Refinished By" section.

1st Type of Covering (paint, paper, etc.) _____

Purchased From _____ Date _____

   Brand & Pattern _____

   Color & No. _____ Warranty Period _____

   Cost/Unit $_____ No. of Units _____ Total $_____

Installed By _____

   Date _____ Cost $_____

Notes: _____

_____

2nd Type of Covering (woodwork, paneling, etc.) _____

Purchased From _____ Date _____

   Brand & Pattern _____

   Color & No. _____ Warranty Period _____

   Cost/Unit $_____ No. of Units _____ Total $_____

Installed By _____

   Date _____ Cost $_____

Refinished By _____

   Date _____ Cost $_____

Notes: _____

_____

SAMPLES: PAINT, WALLPAPER, ETC.

attach swatch or paint daub here

80

DOORS/TRIM

Purchased From _____ Date _____

    Brand & Style _____ Material (oak, steel, etc.)_____

    Stain/Paint Color & No. _____

       Finished With (polyurethane over stain, etc.) _____

Installed By _____ Total Cost $_____

Refinished By _____

    Refinished With _____

    Date _____ Cost $_____

Hardware Description _____

_____

    Purchased From _____ Date _____

    Cost/Unit $_____ No. of Units _____ Total $_____

Notes: _____

_____

FURNITURE/FIXTURES

Item	Purchased From	Date	Cost	Warranty

EXTRA NOTES
(Use tick marks at top & bottom to make graph paper)

MISCELLANEOUS ROOM I

FLOOR COVERING

Floor Measurements

Widest part of room from middle of doorway _____

Longest part of room from middle of doorway _____

Notes: _____

_____

Type & Material (nylon carpet, ceramic tile, etc.) _____

Purchased From _____ Date _____

Brand & Pattern _____

Color & No. _____ Warranty Period _____

Type of Backing _____ Pad Type _____

Cost/Unit $_____ No. of Units _____ Total $_____

Installed By _____ Attached With _____

Date _____ Cost $_____

Cleaned/Refinished By _____

Date 1 _____ Cost $_____

Date 2 _____ Cost $_____

Date 3 _____ Cost $_____

Notes: _____

_____

CEILING COVERING

Type of Covering (paint, spray texture, etc.) _____

Purchased From _____ Date _____

Brand & Pattern _____

Color & No. _____ Warranty Period _____

Applied with (texture roller, sprayer, etc.) _____

Cost/Unit $_____ No. of Units _____ Total $_____

Installed By _____

Date _____ Cost $_____

Notes: _____

_____

WINDOW COVERING

Window 1 Measurements

Height _____ Width _____ Top of Window to Floor _____ Trim Width _____

Type of Covering (draperies, blinds, etc.) _____

Purchased From _____ Cost $_____ Date _____

   Measurements of Window Covering _____

   Material & Cleaning Instructions _____

Cleaned By _____ Cost $_____ Date _____

Cleaned By _____ Cost $_____ Date _____

Notes: _____

_____

_____

Window 2 Measurements

Height _____ Width _____ Top of Window to Floor _____ Trim Width _____

Type of Covering (draperies, blinds, etc.) _____

Purchased From _____ Cost $_____ Date _____

   Measurements of Window Covering _____

   Material & Cleaning Instructions _____

Cleaned By _____ Cost $_____ Date _____

Notes: _____

_____

Window 3 Measurements

Height _____ Width _____ Top of Window to Floor _____ Trim Width _____

Type of Covering (draperies, blinds, etc.) _____

Purchased From _____ Cost $_____ Date _____

   Measurements of Window Covering _____

   Material & Cleaning Instructions _____

Cleaned By _____ Cost $_____ Date _____

Notes: _____

_____

WALL COVERING

Wall Measurements

North _____ South _____ East _____ West _____

Use "2nd Type of Covering" for woodwork or paneling. It has a "Refinished By" section.

1st Type of Covering (paint, paper, etc.) _____

Purchased From _____ Date _____

Brand & Pattern _____

Color & No. _____ Warranty Period _____

Cost/Unit $_____ No. of Units _____ Total $_____

Installed By _____

Date _____ Cost $_____

Notes: _____

_____

2nd Type of Covering (woodwork, paneling, etc.) _____

Purchased From _____ Date _____

Brand & Pattern _____

Color & No. _____ Warranty Period _____

Cost/Unit $_____ No. of Units _____ Total $_____

Installed By _____

Date _____ Cost $_____

Refinished By _____

Date _____ Cost $_____

Notes: _____

_____

SAMPLES: PAINT, WALLPAPER, ETC.

attach swatch or paint daub here

DOORS/TRIM

Purchased From _____ Date _____

    Brand & Style _____ Material (oak, steel, etc.)_____

    Stain/Paint Color & No. _____

    Finished With (polyurethane over stain, etc.) _____

Installed By _____ Total Cost $_____

Refinished By _____

    Refinished With _____

    Date _____ Cost $_____

Hardware Description _____

_____

    Purchased From _____ Date _____

    Cost/Unit $_____ No. of Units _____ Total $_____

Notes: _____

_____

FURNITURE/FIXTURES

Item	Purchased From	Date	Cost	Warranty

EXTRA NOTES
(Use tick marks at top & bottom to make graph paper)

MISCELLANEOUS ROOM 2

FLOOR COVERING

Floor Measurements

Widest part of room from middle of doorway _____

Longest part of room from middle of doorway _____

Notes: _____

_____

Type & Material (nylon carpet, ceramic tile, etc.) _____

Purchased From _____ Date _____

   Brand & Pattern _____

   Color & No. _____ Warranty Period _____

   Type of Backing _____ Pad Type _____

   Cost/Unit $_____ No. of Units _____ Total $_____

Installed By _____ Attached With _____

   Date _____ Cost $_____

Cleaned/Refinished By _____

   Date 1 _____ Cost $_____

   Date 2 _____ Cost $_____

   Date 3 _____ Cost $_____

Notes: _____

CEILING COVERING

Type of Covering (paint, spray texture, etc.) _____

Purchased From _____ Date _____

   Brand & Pattern _____

   Color & No. _____ Warranty Period _____

   Applied with (texture roller, sprayer, etc.) _____

   Cost/Unit $_____ No. of Units _____ Total $_____

Installed By _____

   Date _____ Cost $_____

Notes: _____

WINDOW COVERING

Window 1 Measurements

Height _____ Width _____ Top of Window to Floor _____ Trim Width _____

Type of Covering (draperies, blinds, etc.) _____

Purchased From _____ Cost $_____ Date _____

    Measurements of Window Covering _____

    Material & Cleaning Instructions _____

Cleaned By _____ Cost $_____ Date _____

Cleaned By _____ Cost $_____ Date _____

Notes: _____

_____

_____

Window 2 Measurements

Height _____ Width _____ Top of Window to Floor _____ Trim Width _____

Type of Covering (draperies, blinds, etc.) _____

Purchased From _____ Cost $_____ Date _____

    Measurements of Window Covering _____

    Material & Cleaning Instructions _____

Cleaned By _____ Cost $_____ Date _____

Notes: _____

_____

Window 3 Measurements

Height _____ Width _____ Top of Window to Floor _____ Trim Width _____

Type of Covering (draperies, blinds, etc.) _____

Purchased From _____ Cost $_____ Date _____

    Measurements of Window Covering _____

    Material & Cleaning Instructions _____

Cleaned By _____ Cost $_____ Date _____

Notes: _____

_____

WALL COVERING
<u>**Wall Measurements**</u>

North _____ South _____ East _____ West _____

Use "2nd Type of Covering" for woodwork or paneling. It has a "Refinished By" section.

1st **Type of Covering** (paint, paper, etc.) _____

Purchased From _____ Date _____

    Brand & Pattern _____

    Color & No. _____ Warranty Period _____

    Cost/Unit $_____ No. of Units _____ Total $_____

Installed By _____

    Date _____ Cost $_____

Notes: _____

_____

2nd **Type of Covering** (woodwork, paneling, etc.) _____

Purchased From _____ Date _____

    Brand & Pattern _____

    Color & No. _____ Warranty Period _____

    Cost/Unit $_____ No. of Units _____ Total $_____

Installed By _____

    Date _____ Cost $_____

Refinished By _____

    Date _____ Cost $_____

Notes: _____

_____

SAMPLES: PAINT, WALLPAPER, ETC.

attach swatch or paint daub here

DOORS/TRIM

Purchased From _____ Date _____

    Brand & Style _____ Material (oak, steel, etc.)_____

    Stain/Paint Color & No. _____

        Finished With (polyurethane over stain, etc.) _____

Installed By _____ Total Cost $_____

Refinished By _____

    Refinished With _____

    Date _____ Cost $_____

Hardware Description _____

_____

    Purchased From _____ Date _____

    Cost/Unit $_____ No. of Units _____ Total $_____

Notes: _____

FURNITURE/FIXTURES

Item	Purchased From	Date	Cost	Warranty

EXTRA NOTES
(Use tick marks at top & bottom to make graph paper)

MISCELLANEOUS ROOM 3

FLOOR COVERING

Floor Measurements

Widest part of room from middle of doorway _____

Longest part of room from middle of doorway _____

Notes: _____

_____

Type & Material (nylon carpet, ceramic tile, etc.) _____

Purchased From _____ Date _____

Brand & Pattern _____

Color & No. _____ Warranty Period _____

Type of Backing _____ Pad Type _____

Cost/Unit $_____ No. of Units _____ Total $_____

Installed By _____ Attached With _____

Date _____ Cost $_____

Cleaned/Refinished By _____

Date 1 _____ Cost $_____

Date 2 _____ Cost $_____

Date 3 _____ Cost $_____

Notes: _____

_____

CEILING COVERING

Type of Covering (paint, spray texture, etc.) _____

Purchased From _____ Date _____

Brand & Pattern _____

Color & No. _____ Warranty Period _____

Applied with (texture roller, sprayer, etc.) _____

Cost/Unit $_____ No. of Units _____ Total $_____

Installed By _____

Date _____ Cost $_____

Notes: _____

_____

WINDOW COVERING

Window 1 Measurements

Height _____ Width _____ Top of Window to Floor _____ Trim Width _____

Type of Covering (draperies, blinds, etc.) _____

Purchased From _____ Cost $_____ Date _____

   Measurements of Window Covering _____

   Material & Cleaning Instructions _____

Cleaned By _____ Cost $_____ Date _____

Cleaned By _____ Cost $_____ Date _____

Notes: _____

_____

_____

Window 2 Measurements

Height _____ Width _____ Top of Window to Floor _____ Trim Width _____

Type of Covering (draperies, blinds, etc.) _____

Purchased From _____ Cost $_____ Date _____

   Measurements of Window Covering _____

   Material & Cleaning Instructions _____

Cleaned By _____ Cost $_____ Date _____

Notes: _____

_____

Window 3 Measurements

Height _____ Width _____ Top of Window to Floor _____ Trim Width _____

Type of Covering (draperies, blinds, etc.) _____

Purchased From _____ Cost $_____ Date _____

   Measurements of Window Covering _____

   Material & Cleaning Instructions _____

Cleaned By _____ Cost $_____ Date _____

Notes: _____

_____

WALL COVERING

<u>Wall Measurements</u>

North _____ South _____ East _____ West _____

Use "2nd Type of Covering" for woodwork or paneling. It has a "Refinished By" section.

1st Type of Covering (paint, paper, etc.) _____

Purchased From _____ Date _____

    Brand & Pattern _____

    Color & No. _____ Warranty Period _____

    Cost/Unit $_____ No. of Units _____ Total $_____

Installed By _____

    Date _____ Cost $_____

Notes: _____

_____

2nd Type of Covering (woodwork, paneling, etc.) _____

Purchased From _____ Date _____

    Brand & Pattern _____

    Color & No. _____ Warranty Period _____

    Cost/Unit $_____ No. of Units _____ Total $_____

Installed By _____

    Date _____ Cost $_____

Refinished By _____

    Date _____ Cost $_____

Notes: _____

_____

SAMPLES: PAINT, WALLPAPER, ETC.

attach swatch or paint daub here

DOORS/TRIM

Purchased From _____ Date _____

   Brand & Style _____ Material (oak, steel, etc.)_____

   Stain/Paint Color & No. _____

     Finished With (polyurethane over stain, etc.) _____

Installed By _____ Total Cost $_____

Refinished By _____

   Refinished With _____

   Date _____ Cost $_____

Hardware Description _____

_____

   Purchased From _____ Date _____

   Cost/Unit $_____ No. of Units _____ Total $_____

Notes: _____

_____

FURNITURE/FIXTURES

Item	Purchased From	Date	Cost	Warranty

EXTRA NOTES

(Use tick marks at top & bottom to make graph paper)

93

STORAGE/CLOSETS

DECK

Type of Wood (redwood, green treated, etc.) _____

Purchased From _____ Date _____

Sealed/Finished With (brand, type, color, no.) _____

Misc. Materials _____ Cost $_____

Installed By _____ Total $_____

Refinished With _____ Date _____

    Contractor _____ Cost $_____

Refinished With _____ Date _____

    Contractor _____ Cost $_____

Refinished With _____ Date _____

    Contractor _____ Cost $_____

Notes: _____

_____

_____

DRIVEWAY

Type of Driveway (asphalt, concrete, etc.) _____

Installed By _____ Cost $_____ Date _____

Sealed With (brand, type, & no.) _____

    Purchased From/Contractor _____ Date _____

    Cost/Unit $_____ No. of Units _____ Total $_____

Sealed With (brand, type, & no.) _____

    Purchased From/Contractor _____ Date _____

    Cost/Unit $_____ No. of Units _____ Total $_____

Sealed With (brand, type, & no.) _____

    Purchased From/Contractor _____ Date _____

    Cost/Unit $_____ No. of Units _____ Total $_____

Sealed With (brand, type, & no.) _____

    Purchased From/Contractor _____ Date _____

    Cost/Unit $_____ No. of Units _____ Total $_____

    Notes: _____

_____

_____

FENCES

1st Fence Type of Material (redwood, wire, etc.) _____

Purchased From _____ Date _____

Finished With (brand, type, color, no.) _____

Installed By _____ Total $_____ Date _____

Refinished With _____ Date _____

   Contractor _____ Cost $_____

Refinished With _____ Date _____

   Contractor _____ Cost $_____

Notes: _____

_____

_____

_____

2nd Fence Type of Material (redwood, wire, etc.) _____

Purchased From _____ Date _____

Finished With (brand, type, color, no.) _____

Installed By _____ Total $_____ Date _____

Refinished With _____ Date _____

   Contractor _____ Cost $_____

Refinished With _____ Date _____

   Contractor _____ Cost $_____

Notes: _____

_____

_____

_____

GAZEBO

_____

_____

_____

_____

_____

_____

_____

PATIO

Type of Material (patio blocks, cement, etc.) _____

Installed By _____ Total $_____ Date _____

Sealed With (brand, type, & no.) _____

    Contractor _____ Cost $_____ Date _____

Sealed With (brand, type, & no.) _____

    Contractor _____ Cost $_____ Date _____

Notes: _____

_____

PORCH

(Use tick marks at top & bottom to make graph paper)

STORAGE SHEDS/OUTBUILDINGS

GARAGE
FLOOR

Type of Floor (asphalt, concrete, etc.) _____

Installed By _____ Cost $_____ Date _____

Sealed/Finished With (brand, type, & no.) _____

    Purchased From _____ Date _____

    Cost/Unit $_____ No. of Units _____ Total $_____

Maintenance _____

_____

Notes: _____

_____

GUTTERS & DOWNSPOUTS

Type of Material (steel, vinyl, etc.) _____ Warranty Period _____

Purchased From _____ Date _____

Cost/Unit $_____ No. of Units _____ Total $_____

Installed By _____ Cost $_____ Date _____

Notes: _____

_____

_____

ROOF

Type of Roofing (fiberglass shingles, cedar shakes, etc.) _____

Purchased From _____ Date _____ Warranty Period _____

    Brand, Color & No. _____

    Cost/Unit $_____ No. of Units _____ Total $_____

Misc. Materials _____ Cost $_____

Installed By _____ Cost $_____ Date _____

Total Materials Cost $ _____ Entire Job Cost $_____

Maintenance (preservative, repairs, etc.) _____

_____

Notes: _____

_____

_____

SIDING

1st Type of Siding (brick, stucco, etc.) _____

Supplier _____ Date _____ Warranty Period _____

   Brand, Color, & No. _____

   Cost/Unit $_____ No. of Units _____ Total $_____

Type of Finish (paint, stain, etc.) _____

   Cost/Unit $_____ No. of Units _____ Total $_____

   Purchased From _____ Date _____ Warranty Period _____

Installed By _____ Cost $_____ Date _____

Notes: _____

   _____

   _____

   _____

   _____

   _____

   _____

2nd Type of Siding (brick, stucco, etc.) _____

Supplier _____ Date _____ Warranty Period _____

   Brand, Color, & No. _____

   Cost/Unit $_____ No. of Units _____ Total $_____

Type of Finish (paint, stain, etc.) _____

   Cost/Unit $_____ No. of Units _____ Total $_____

   Purchased From _____ Date _____ Warranty Period _____

Installed By _____ Cost $_____ Date _____

Notes: _____

_____

_____

_____

_____

_____

_____

_____

TRIM

<u>1st Type of Trim</u> (wood, vinyl, etc.) _____

Supplier _____ Date _____ Warranty Period _____

    Brand, Color, & No. _____

    Cost/Unit $_____ No. of Units _____ Total $_____

Type of Finish (paint, stain, etc.) _____

    Cost/Unit $_____ No. of Units _____ Total $_____

    Purchased From _____ Date _____ Warranty Period _____

Installed By _____ Cost $_____ Date _____

Notes: _____

_____

_____

<u>2nd Type of Trim</u> (wood, vinyl, etc.) _____

Supplier _____ Date _____ Warranty Period _____

    Brand, Color, & No. _____

    Cost/Unit $_____ No. of Units _____ Total $_____

Type of Finish (paint, stain, etc.) _____

    Cost/Unit $_____ No. of Units _____ Total $_____

    Purchased From _____ Date _____ Warranty Period _____

Installed By _____ Cost $_____ Date _____

Notes: _____

WALLS & CEILING

<u>Type of Material</u> (gypsum board, etc.) _____

Purchased From _____ Date _____ Warranty Period _____

    Cost/Unit $_____ No. of Units _____ Total $_____

    Sealed/Finished With (brand, color, & no.) _____

Notes: _____

_____

_____

HOUSE EXTERIOR
GUTTERS & DOWNSPOUTS

Type of Material (steel, vinyl, etc.) _____ Warranty Period _____

Purchased From _____ Date _____

Cost/Unit $_____ No. of Units _____ Total $_____

Installed By _____ Cost $_____ Date _____

Notes: _____

_____

_____

_____

_____

_____

ROOF

Type of Roofing (fiberglass shingles, cedar shakes, etc.) _____

Purchased From _____ Date _____ Warranty Period _____

Brand, Color & No. _____

Cost/Unit $_____ No. of Units _____ Total $_____

Misc. Materials _____ Cost $_____

Installed By _____ Cost $_____ Date _____

Total Materials Cost $ _____ Entire Job Cost $_____

Maintenance (preservative, repairs, etc.) _____

_____

_____

Notes: _____

_____

_____

STORM DOORS

_____

_____

_____

_____

_____

SIDING

1st Type of Siding (brick, stucco, etc.) _____

Supplier _____ Date _____ Warranty Period _____

   Brand, Color, & No. _____

   Cost/Unit $_____ No. of Units _____ Total $_____

Type of Finish (paint, stain, etc.) _____

   Cost/Unit $_____ No. of Units _____ Total $_____

   Purchased From _____ Date _____ Warranty Period _____

Installed By _____ Cost $_____ Date _____

Notes: _____

_____

_____

2nd Type of Siding (brick, stucco, etc.) _____

Supplier _____ Date _____ Warranty Period _____

   Brand, Color, & No. _____

   Cost/Unit $_____ No. of Units _____ Total $_____

Type of Finish (paint, stain, etc.) _____

   Cost/Unit $_____ No. of Units _____ Total $_____

   Purchased From _____ Date _____ Warranty Period _____

Installed By _____ Cost $_____ Date _____

Notes: _____

_____

_____

STORM WINDOWS

Type of Frame (wood, vinyl, etc.) _____

(Use "Trim" on next page for "Type of Finish")

Purchased From _____ Date _____ Warranty Period _____

   Cost/Unit $_____ No. of Units _____ Total $_____

Installed By _____ Cost $_____ Date _____

Notes: _____

_____

_____

TRIM

1st Type of Trim (wood, vinyl, etc.) _____

Supplier _____ Date _____ Warranty Period _____

   Brand, Color, & No. _____

   Cost/Unit $_____ No. of Units _____ Total $_____

Type of Finish (paint, stain, etc.) _____

   Cost/Unit $_____ No. of Units _____ Total $_____

   Purchased From _____ Date _____ Warranty Period _____

Installed By _____ Cost $_____ Date _____

Notes: _____

_____

_____

_____

2nd Type of Trim (wood, vinyl, etc.) _____

Supplier _____ Date _____ Warranty Period _____

   Brand, Color, & No. _____

   Cost/Unit $_____ No. of Units _____ Total $_____

Type of Finish (paint, stain, etc.) _____

   Cost/Unit $_____ No. of Units _____ Total $_____

   Purchased From _____ Date _____ Warranty Period _____

Installed By _____ Cost $_____ Date _____

Notes: _____

_____

_____

EXTRA NOTES

_____

_____

_____

_____

_____

COOLING & HEATING
AIR CONDITIONER

Type of Unit (electric, natural gas, etc.) _____

Manufacturer & Model _____ Efficiency _____

Purchased From/Contractor _____ Date _____

    Cost $_____ Warranty Period _____

    Filter Type _____ Size _____

Cleaned/Serviced By _____

    Date No. 1 _____ Cost $_____

    Date No. 2 _____ Cost $_____

    Date No. 3 _____ Cost $_____

    Date No. 4 _____ Cost $_____

Notes: _____

FIREPLACE

Insert Mfr. & Model _____

Purchased From _____ Date _____

    Cost $_____ Warranty Period _____

Installed By _____ Cost $_____ Date _____

Chimney Cleaned By _____

    Date No. 1 _____ Cost $_____

    Date No. 2 _____ Cost $_____

Notes: _____

HEAT EXCHANGER

Manufacturer & Model _____ Efficiency _____

Purchased From _____ Date _____

    Cost $_____ Warranty Period _____

Installed By _____ Cost $_____ Date _____

Cleaned/Serviced By _____ Cost $_____ Date _____

Notes: _____

HEAT PUMP

Type of Unit (electric, fuel oil, etc.) _____

Manufacturer & Model _____ Efficiency _____

Purchased From/Contractor _____ Date _____

    Cost $_____ Warranty Period _____

    Filter Type _____ Size _____

Cleaned/Serviced By _____

    Date No. 1 _____ Cost $_____

    Date No. 2 _____ Cost $_____

Notes: _____

HEATING PLANT (Furnace)

Type of Unit (electric, fuel oil, etc.) _____

Manufacturer & Model _____ Efficiency _____

Purchased From/Contractor _____ Date _____

    Cost $_____ Warranty Period _____

    Filter Type _____ Size _____

    Humidifier _____

Cleaned/Serviced By _____

    Date No. 1 _____ Cost $_____

    Date No. 2 _____ Cost $_____

    Date No. 3 _____ Cost $_____

    Date No. 4 _____ Cost $_____

Notes: _____

WOOD STOVE

Manufacturer & Model _____ Efficiency _____

Purchased From/Contractor _____ Date _____

    Cost $_____ Warranty Period _____

Chimney Cleaned By _____

    Date No. 1 _____ Cost $_____

    Date No. 2 _____ Cost $_____

Notes: _____

INSULATION
ATTIC

Type of Insulation (fiberglass rolls, etc.) _____

    Thickness _____ R-Value Added _____ Cost $_____

    Previous R-Value _____ Aggregate R-Value _____

    Type of Vapor Barrier (6 mill poly, etc.) _____

Installed By _____ Date _____

Total Material Cost $_____ Labor $_____ Total $_____

Notes: _____

_____

_____

Type of Venting   Note: You should have one square foot of free-flowing cross-ventilation for every 150 square feet. of attic floor space. Soffit vents with screen covers can reduce air flow by up to 75%.

Under Eave (Soffit) Sq. In./cm _____ Louvered Attic Vents Sq. In./cm _____

Low Pitch Slant Roof Vents Sq. In./cm _____ Turbines Sq. In./cm _____

Other _____

    Notes: _____

_____

WALLS

1ˢᵗ Type of Insulation (fiberglass rolls, etc.) _____

    Thickness _____ R-Value Added _____ Cost $_____

2nd Type of Insulation (fiberglass rolls, etc.) _____

    Thickness _____ R-Value Added _____ Cost $_____

Aggregate R-Value _____ Warranty Period _____

Type of Vapor Barrier (6 mill poly, etc.) _____

Installed By _____ Date _____

Total Material Cost $_____ Labor $_____ Total $_____

Notes: _____

_____

_____

_____

OTHER INSULATION
(rim joist, exterior foundation, etc.)

DOOR CHIMES

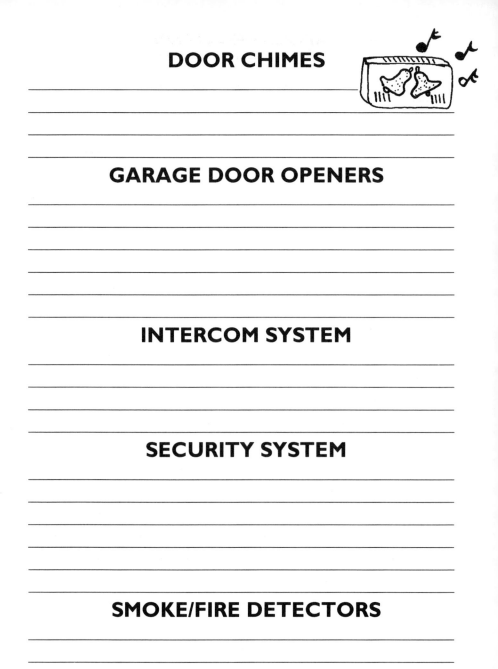

_____
_____
_____
_____

GARAGE DOOR OPENERS

_____
_____
_____
_____
_____
_____

INTERCOM SYSTEM

_____
_____
_____
_____

SECURITY SYSTEM

_____
_____
_____
_____
_____
_____

SMOKE/FIRE DETECTORS

_____
_____
_____
_____
_____
_____
_____

TELEPHONES/ANSWERING MACHINE/FAX

_____
_____
_____
_____
_____
_____
_____

THERMOSTATS

_____
_____
_____
_____

RADON TESTING & INFORMATION

_____
_____
_____
_____

SEWER/CESSPOOL/SEPTIC SYSTEM

_____
_____
_____
_____
_____

SUMP PUMP

_____
_____

SWIMMING POOL

WATER HEATERS

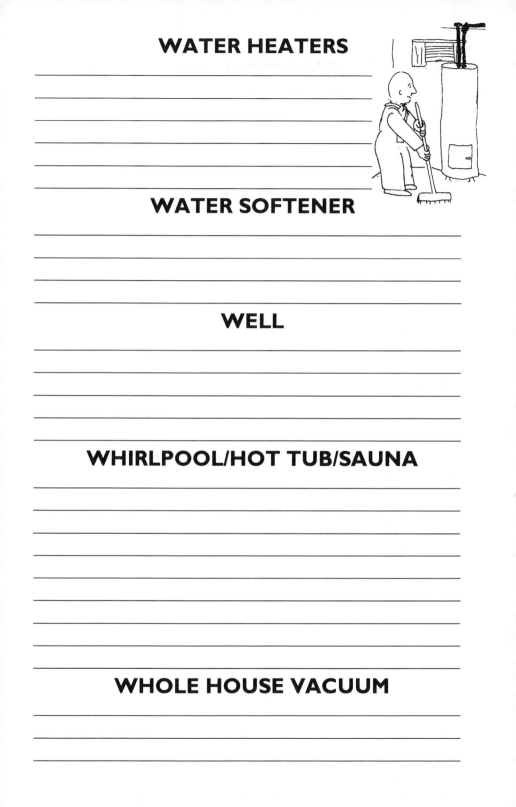

_____
_____
_____
_____
_____
_____

WATER SOFTENER

_____
_____
_____
_____

WELL

_____
_____
_____
_____

WHIRLPOOL/HOT TUB/SAUNA

_____
_____
_____
_____
_____
_____
_____

WHOLE HOUSE VACUUM

_____
_____
_____

GARDENING/LANDSCAPING
GARDEN DIARY/PHENOLOGY

(Record special events or occurrences around your home, such as the all-time earliest day you've ever sighted a robin, or picked that first tomato of the season. If you live in a colder climate, you might want to record the largest snowfall. Use pencil to allow for easy updates)

1st/Earliest _____

1st/Earliest _____

Last _____

Last _____

Most rain _____

Heat wave/highest temp. _____

Cold wave/coldest temp. _____

Last snow/most snow _____

Record vegetable size or harvest _____

_____

Bird sightings _____

_____

_____

_____

Wildlife sightings _____

_____

_____

Other _____

_____

_____

_____

_____

_____

_____

_____

_____

_____

_____

GARDEN/YARD DIAGRAMS

(Use tick marks on lines to make graph paper to create one large diagram, or a few small diagrams for individual flowerbeds. Use any leftover space for notes.)

TREES/SHRUBS/PERENNIALS

Plant Type	Size	Qty.	Cost	Date	Supplier

Special Care/Notes: _____

Special Care/Notes: _____

Special Care/Notes: _____

Special Care/Notes: _____

Special Care/Notes: _____

Special Care/Notes: _____

Plant Type	Size	Qty.	Cost	Date	Supplier

Special Care/Notes: _____

Special Care/Notes: _____

Special Care/Notes: _____

Special Care/Notes: _____

Special Care/Notes: _____

Special Care/Notes: _____

WATERFALL/WATER GARDEN/FOUNTAIN

Type (waterfall, self-contained fountain, etc.) _____

Material	Qty.	Cost	Date	Warranty	Supplier

Pump _____ Size _____ Cost _____ Date _____ Warranty _____

Electrical/Lights _____

Purchased from _____ Cost _____ Date _____ Warranty _____

Installed by _____ Cost _____ Date _____

Cleaning _____

Chemical Treatment _____

Maintenance _____

Plant Type	Qty.	Cost	Date	Supplier

Fish Type	Size	Qty.	Cost	Date	Supplier

EQUIPMENT

(Tractors, mowers, snow blowers, etc.)

Type _____ Mfr. _____ Model _____ Serial No. _____

Purchased From _____ Cost _____ Date _____ Warranty _____

Maintenance/Service _____

_____

_____

_____

Notes: _____

_____

Type _____ Mfr. _____ Model _____ Serial No. _____

Purchased From _____ Cost _____ Date _____ Warranty _____

Maintenance/Service _____

_____

_____

_____

Notes: _____

_____

Type _____ Mfr. _____ Model _____ Serial No. _____

Purchased From _____ Cost _____ Date _____ Warranty _____

Maintenance/Service _____

_____

_____

_____

Notes: _____

_____

Type _____ Mfr. _____ Model _____ Serial No. _____

Purchased From _____ Cost _____ Date _____ Warranty _____

Maintenance/Service _____

_____

_____

_____

Notes: _____

PORTABLE (luggable) ITEMS

ARBOR/TRELLIS/LATTICE

_____

_____

BARBEQUE/GRILL

_____

_____

BIRD FEEDERS & BATHS/WILDLIFE FEEDERS

_____

_____

_____

_____

COMPOST BIN

_____

LAWN FURNITURE/PICNIC TABLE

_____

_____

_____

LAWN SWING/GLIDER

_____

_____

LIGHTING-OUTDOOR

_____

_____

_____

_____

ORNAMENTS/STATUARY/FLOWER BOXES

RETAINING WALLS

(The tick marks at top & bottom can be used to make graph paper to diagram walls)

SWING & PLAY SETS/SAND BOX

WHEELBARROWS/CARTS/PLANTING TABLES

YARD TOOLS/EQUIPMENT

LAWN/GARDEN IRRIGATION & SERVICE

GARDEN IRRIGATION

(The tick marks at top & bottom can be used to make graph paper to diagram system)

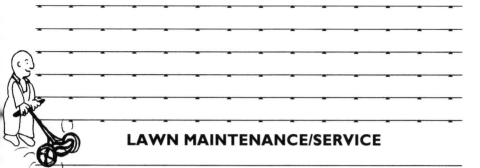

LAWN MAINTENANCE/SERVICE

SPRINKLER SYSTEM

(The tick marks at top & bottom can be used to make graph paper to diagram system)

WATERING SCHEDULE

GARDEN/YARD MISCELLANEOUS

BURIED CABLE/PIPELINE LOCATIONS

EDGING

MULCH

PESTS (insects, animals, not neighbors)

SOIL SAMPLES

WEED BARRIER

TAX IMPLICATIONS OF
SELLING YOUR HOME

Notice: *This is a general overview of the tax concepts to consider when buying and selling your principal residence. It is not intended to be a complete discussion of all the tax implications of selling your home, which vary regionally. If you have any questions, seek the advice of a qualified tax professional.*

You can generally exclude from income up to $250,000 of gain ($500,000 for joint filers) from the sale of the home that you own and have used as your principal residence for at least 2 of the 5 years before the sale. The full exclusion doesn't apply if, within the 2-year period ending on the sale date, you had another home sale to which the exclusion applied. However, a partial exclusion may apply if you must sell your home due to a change of place of employment, health, or to other unforeseen circumstances.

In the event that you do not qualify for the capital gain exclusion, you can still minimize your income taxes by keeping the proper information to calculate the tax basis of your home. The tax basis of your home is the amount paid for your home plus miscellaneous costs associated with the purchase of a home (appraisal fees, title cost, etc.), plus subsequent improvements.

Subsequent improvements include items such as finishing the basement, adding additional rooms, replacing the furnace, installing an air conditioning system, replacing the roof, landscaping, fencing, swimming pools, etc. Repairs, on the other hand, are not included in the tax basis of your home. Repairs include items such as painting, re-coating the driveway, replacing broken windows, repairing or replacing electrical fixtures, etc. However, if repairs were done as part of a larger renovation of your home, they would be included in the renovation costs and could then be added to the tax basis.

In calculating the tax basis of your home, include the original cost of your home plus any subsequent improvements. When you sell your home, the Internal Revenue Service requires that you have sufficient documentation to substantiate the tax basis. Sufficient documentation includes the closing papers on the purchase of your home and invoices and receipts for any improvements you made. You will need the invoices from the contractors showing the date the improvements were made, what was done, and how much it cost. If you do the work yourself, you will need to keep receipts for materials. Also, if you do the work yourself, you cannot add your own labor to the tax basis.

The following pages are included to record the improvements made to your home. When an improvement is made, record the date, description, and amount. Remember that you need to keep the supporting documentation (invoices and receipts) to substantiate these items.

Special thanks for this tax information goes to the certified public accounting firm of Mathwig & Whipps, P.A., located in Apple Valley, Minnesota.

TAX WORKSHEET

Amount

Original Cost of Home Per Purchase Agreement _____

Add Closing Costs:

Legal Fees _____

Appraisal Fee _____

Commission Fee to Broker _____

Escrow Fee _____

Title Cost _____

State Deed Taxes and Filing Fees _____

Loan Placement Fees (e.g. Points) _____

Other _____

Add Remodeling and Renovations Made:

Date	Description	Amount

Add Improvements Made:

Date   Description   Amount

_____

_____

_____

_____

_____

_____

_____

_____

_____

_____

_____

_____

_____

_____

_____

_____

_____

_____

_____

_____

_____

_____

_____

_____

_____

HOW TO FILE IMPORTANT PAPERS

Every home owner needs a good home filing system for keeping important documents and receipts for tax, insurance, warranty, or budget purposes. A good system will also save you a great deal of money, time, and aggravation. Take time in the beginning to set up the system that is right for you. The right system will be easy to use and allow for easy retrieval of documents. A system that is too primitive is no better than throwing all receipts into a shoebox. Conversely, a filing system that is too complex will be a chore to use.

After considerable research and experimentation, I developed a filing system that is easy to use, easy on my time, flexible, and inexpensive to start. All it consists of is:

1. Two large expanding folders with individual pockets and preprinted alphabetic tabs: (a) one set is for filing papers dealing with the purchase of your home and any work done on your home and (b) the other set is to file receipts for things you buy for your home and family. These separate folders eliminate what could be a huge sorting problem when tax information must be separated from ordinary purchases.

2. A household inventory for insurance purposes.

The supplies for this system are inexpensive, especially when compared to the money, time, and patience you may lose without them. They are available in many book, office supply, and variety stores.

Label one expanding folder "Home Owner's Journal." This set is for filing papers dealing with the **purchase of your home** and any **work done on your home**. Keep only photocopies of important receipts in this file (put the originals in your safe-deposit box). Include receipts for budgeting, planning, and tax purposes (see the Tax Implications of Selling Your Home chapter). This file should also contain copies of purchase agreements and other closing documents from the purchase your home, receipts for repairs, additions, installation, purchases, care or cleaning instructions, contractor business cards, etc.

File each item under the appropriate letter in the alphabet. For example, living room carpet receipts, warranties, care instructions, the installer's business card, etc. should be stapled together, labeled "living room carpet," and filed under "C" for carpet. Don't forget to make appropriate notes on the documents such as "date purchased" if they are not already marked.

If you are not sure where to file something, put it in the most obvious place and put a "See _____" cross-reference note where it could also be filed. Periodically purge the file of information you no longer need, such as expired warranties and receipts for old paint you wallpapered over.

The second expanding folder should be labeled "Purchases." This set is for all the receipts, care and cleaning instructions, warranty cards, serial numbers, and instruction booklets for things you buy for your home and family such as appliances, electronics, furniture, wrist watches, etc. File each of these items under the appropriate letter of the alphabet. Follow the same filing instructions as in the previous paragraphs.

It is a good idea to maintain a written inventory of the contents of your home for insurance purposes in case of fire or burglary. A written inventory is perhaps easiest done with a good home inventory journal that can be found in book, office supply, and variety stores. Look for one that allows you some flexibility. Many books are so specific that much of the book is wasted with items that don't apply to you. Some can also leave you short of room for the things you do have. If you are very thorough, a tablet will also work.

Photographs or a video tape are good complements, too, but not substitutes for the written inventory. They help show the condition of the item, which is important if you have an "actual cash value" insurance policy (which is often based on the depreciated value) instead of the "replacement value." Ask your insurance agent which type you have. The difference in your premium may not be that much and replacement cost is often well worth the difference.

Another alternative to paper is a tape recorder. As with video tape, however, updates are difficult to make unless added to the end of the tape.

Whichever method you choose, make sure it fits into your safe-deposit box. That is where you should keep it once it is complete. Update it whenever necessary, but return it when finished. Keep a copy at home for reference.

EXTRA NOTES

(Use tick marks at top & bottom to make graph paper)

EXTRA NOTES

(Use tick marks at top & bottom to make graph paper)

EXTRA NOTES

(Use tick marks at top & bottom to make graph paper)

EXTRA NOTES

(Use tick marks at top & bottom to make graph paper)

EXTRA NOTES

(Use tick marks at top & bottom to make graph paper)

INDEX

133